MOBILE MULTIMEDIA IN ACTION

MOBILE MULTIMEDIA IN ACTION

Ilpo Kalevi Koskinen

Transaction Publishers
New Brunswick (U.S.A.) and London (U.K.)

Library of Congress Catalog Number: 2007011677
ISBN: 978-0-7658-0373-3
Printed in the United States of America

Library of Congress Cataloging-in-Publication Data

Koskinen, Ilpo Kalevi.
  Mobile multimedia in action / Ilpo Kalevi Koskinen.
    p. cm.
  Includes bibliographical references and index.
  ISBN 978-0-7658-0373-3
  1. Information technology—Social aspects. 2. Interpersonal communication—Technological innovations—Social aspects.
  3. Cellular tele phones—Social aspects. 4. Mobile communication systems—Social aspects. I. Title.

HM851.K67 2007
303.48'33—dc22   2007011677

Contents

Messages

Tables

Figures

Preface

This volume is my attempt to understand how people use camera phones in communication and action. The roots of this work are in classic ethnomethodology, which I learned through conversation analysis and phenomenology.

The primary aim of the book is not theoretical. However, it tries to articulate one perspective to mobile multimedia as clearly as possible. Five years ago, James E. Katz and Mark Aakhus lamented in *Perpetual Contact,* a volume that has become standard reference in studies of mobile telephony, that studies of mobile telephony had by then created little theory. Of course, they were correct. Theory should be the aim of all research: ultimately, it is only through theoretical discussion that we learn which arguments and perspectives are helpful for us in making sense of things taking place around us. What I have tried to do in this book is to put forth an interpretation that, hopefully, will provoke other people to put forth their own arguments and perspectives. To me, the book is a step in the debate that, hopefully, one day will lead to improved understanding of things taking place in society.

Interpretations like the one I have proposed sometimes have curious careers. The roots of the interpretation go back about seven years to a time when, with the exception of Japan, there were no camera phones on the market. When Nokia released its Communicator (9110), which made it possible to send pictures from one digital camera model by Casio to another phone or to e-mail, I began a study called *Mobile Image* with Esko Kurvinen, an industrial designer, and Turo-Kimmo Lehtonen, a sociologist. When I saw the first messages in this early study, I immediately thought about studying it from an ethnomethodological perspective, which was familiar to me from conversation analysis, an offshoot of ethnomethodology. Seven years later, I am glad to say that this intuition turned out to be productive. This book is my first sustained attempt to show what people do with multimedia messages from an ethnomethodological perspective and to contrast it with other perspectives in literature.

The body of work that has led to this book has aroused interest not only in communication and the social sciences, but also in design and software engineering. In fact, several engineering studies were inspired and provoked by the early phases of this body of work. Since the book attempts not only to explicate multimedia, but also to clarify theory, it will not come as news to some readers in engineering and design, whose minds are in the future rather than on what took place years ago. Still, I hope that they will learn from its details. Primarily, however, I have written the book with sociologists and communication studies researchers in mind. Perhaps it may even create bridges between these disciplines, showing engineers that social scientists can do much with good data, and showing people in the social sciences that working with our more technically minded colleagues can provide an opportunity to get one's hands on wonderfully detailed, technologically and socially relevant data.

Of course, *Mobile Multimedia in Action* is a document from the early years of mobile multimedia. Any attempt to theorize about its impact on society has to be speculative, and needs to be done with more recent data. I decided to explore the relationship of multimedia to society in three particular chapters whose main aims are to give sociologists and other social scientists data to chew on, and the opportunity to see that things of relevance in social terms do take place on the small, colorful screen of the mobile phone. One of the book's main messages is that there is society in technology. It is people who build it into their hi-tech devices while they are doing other, often remarkably ordinary things in everyday life. I hope that it also shows that a persistent, obstinate use of some relatively simple ideas and principles in interpreting data can lead to insights that go far beyond what we see when engaged in our practical concerns.

Acknowledgements

When one writes a book, one inevitably accrues debts to many people. This book is no exception. In particular, I am indebted to Esko Kurvinen and Katja Battarbee, as well as others in what was then known as the Smart Products Research Group at the University of Art and Design Helsinki. Esko and Katja have been working and writing with me for years, and working with them on both sets of data covered in this book has been most enjoyable.

In addition to Esko and Katja, I have to thank Rich Ling, Heidi Rae Cooley, and Ilkka Arminen for reading early versions of the manuscript. Of course, several other people have been helpful in various ways over the last few years. Some have given me opportunities to talk about my observations. Some have shared their ideas with me. Some have opened their technological demonstrations to me. These people include Marc Davis, David Frohlich, Pekka Isomursu, Mimi Ito, Giulio Jacucci, Fumitoshi Kato, Kristof Nyírí, Christian Licoppe, Daisuke Okabe, Kees Overbeeke, Raul Pertierra, Marc Relieu, Carole-Anne Rivière, Petteri Repo, Barbara Scifo, Mirjana Spasojevic, and Nancy van House.

Two conferences in particular have given me new perspectives. The first was the First Asia Europe Conference on Computer Mediated Interactive Communications Technology, Tagaytay City, the Philippines, in October 2003, which served as a wonderful demonstration of the importance of mobile telephony outside the post-industrial world. It was also a truly memorable experience for me. The International Institute for Ethnomethodology and Conversation Analysis at Bentley College, Waltham, Massachusetts, in the United States, in August 2005 gave me an opportunity to explore the body in multimedia messages. I gratefully acknowledge Kees Overbeeke for giving permission to recycle a major portion of a paper I presented at Designing Pleasurable Products and Interfaces in Eindhoven, the Netherlands, in October 2005, which became Chapter 5 of this book.

Irving Louis Horowitz, Mary Curtis, and Larry Mintz from Transaction Publishers were generous enough to publish the book in a series edited by James E. Katz, to whom I am indebted in many ways. He is a fine, open-minded colleague, whose support is always welcomed. I hope James approves what he sees within the covers of this book.

Of the several research assistants with whom I have worked, I want to mention Paula Cabrera Viancha, who did most of the hard work for the *Radiolinja* data set. The Department of Industrial Design has been continuously supportive of me over the years. Work leading to this book has been funded mostly by the Ministry of Trade and Industry of Finland and the mobile carrier Radiolinja (now Elisa). In addition, Nokia Research Center in Tampere, Finland, provided know-how and the Communicators for the *Mobile Image* study.

Above all, of course, I am indebted to those people who participated in the studies leading to this book. In all, forty-five people were involved in the studies, taking pictures, sending pictures, and responding to them.

Part I

Introduction and Theoretical Perspectives

1

Beyond Talk

Mobile Multimedia in Action, which analyzes one of the latest additions to mobile telephony, mobile multimedia, is based on *Mobile Image* and *Radiolinja*, two major studies conducted in Helsinki, Finland, in 1999–2001, both of which are described in detail in the final Chapter. The book probes how people use mobile multimedia as a part of their daily lives to organize their interaction with other people. More specifically, it respecifies mobile multimedia from an ethnomethodological standpoint (Garfinkel 1967, 1996). The central thesis of the analysis is that mobile multimedia cannot be interpreted in terms of a fixed set of needs, functions, and traditional sociological categories such as gender. With these concepts, people become "cultural dopes," driven by something other than their own minds (Garfinkel 1967: 68–69).

By "mobile multimedia," I mean a set of technologies that enable people to capture, send, and receive photographs, sounds, and sometimes video. These devices are small enough to be carried in pockets and handbags, making them perpetually available for communication. Typically, a mobile multimedia device is a mobile telephone with a camera and an audiocapture function. However, PDAs (personal digital assistants) are increasingly converging with mobile phones. The newest PDA models sold primarily in North America have increasingly become like multimedia phones sold in other parts of the world.

Since 2003, mobile multimedia has been the fastest growing segment of the mobile telephone market. In 2004, roughly 200 million digital cameras were sold *in* mobile phones. In the same year, the mobile phone manufacturer Nokia became the largest digital camera manufacturer in the world, selling approximately 60–70 million camera phones. Camera phones are pushing cheaper digital cameras out of the market, much as they earlier displaced alarm clocks, watches, and phone books.

Message 1.1 provides an example of a multimedia message. I received this message from a friend who was in Greece with his family. In essence, the message is a mobile postcard, created and sent with a mobile phone instead of the traditional procedure of buying, writing, and sending a postcard through the post office.

In addition to digital photographs, other types of content that can be communicated with mobile phones include sound files, animations, and video clips. The first experiments with streaming video and mobile television took place early in 2001 and 2002 in several countries like Sweden, Finland, and South Korea (Kasesniemi et al. 2003; Repo et al. 2003; Ok 2005). Similarly, the first experiments with video calls took place in Europe in 2002–2003. In video calls, the interlocutors see each others' faces and, depending on where the camera is pointed, the environment (see O'Hara et al. 2006).

The backdrop of mobile multimedia, of course, is mobile telephony. In less than two decades, mobile phones have become almost ubiquitous.

Message 1.1
Postcard from Greece

Greetings from Greece. Imagine... An old man lives in the upstairs of a windmill Downstairs he has a beach café and sells small snacks. It's really relaxing to be out here. Remember to work hard at work while I'm vacationing... Best wishes, Junior, Mari and kids

The first digital cellular networks became commercially available in the early 1990s, and by the end of 2002, there were more than 1 billion mobile phone users. In 2005, about 700 million handsets were sold. Much like the Internet a few years before, mobile telephony is quickly transforming the world. By 2001, in many countries, with the Asian "tigers" and Scandinavia leading the way, mobile phones had become more common than landline phones and TV sets (Katz and Aakhus 2002: 5; Rice and Katz 2003).

However, mobile telephony is more than just a technological or business success. As Katz and Aakhus (2002: 2–3) note, mobile telephony is a mind-altering and society-altering technology. Many uses of mobile phones are related to managing practical affairs and work (see Rice and Katz 2003; Fortunati 2002) and coordinating actions without clocks and mass media (Ling 2004: 76; Rheingold 2003a). Many other uses of mobile phones are less instrumental: much like personal stereos (Bull 2000), mobile phones fill empty slots with activity and socializing, turning any location into a living room-like place where interaction with friends and acquintances is available at any time (Kopomaa 2000: 14–19). Mobile phones also make it possible for people to be in perpetual contact with acquaintances, friends, and family (Katz and Aakhus 2002; Gergen 2002; Fortunati 2002; Licoppe 2004). Also, some uses are symbolic. Especially among teenagers and young adults, mobile phones have become fashion items with which people construct social identities and define group memberships (Fortunati et al. 2003; Lobet-Maris 2003: 88; Ling 2003: 98; Kasesniemi 2003: 217–238). Mobile phones have changed the ways in which we experience our environment, orient in cities, work, communicate, understand our social environment, and also the way in which we interact.

This phenomenon must be the initial hypothesis for any study on mobile multimedia as well. Mobile multimedia has been a success for handset manufacturers, even though initial evidence from use suggests that people adopt mobile multimedia at a much slower pace than expected. For example, in 2005 in Norway, a country of 4.5 million inhabitants with one of the highest mobile phone penetration rates in the world, people sent 489,000 multimedia messages each day (e-mail, Rich Ling Jan. 2006; for 2002 figures, see Ling 2004: 145). At the same time, 504,000 text messages were sent every hour, making over 12 million daily text messages. The ratio of multimedia messages to text messages is thus only about 1/25. However, as absolute numbers suggest, mobile multimedia is already a significant force in Norwegian society. More than anywhere else, mobile multimedia has been a hit in Japan (Matsunaga 2000; Natsuno 2003; Ratliff 2001; Barnes and Huff 2003; Barry and Yu 2002; Bradley and Sandoval 2002; Ishii 2004; Kusahara 2004), despite the failure of WAP (Teo and Pok 2003a,b; Hung et al. 2003; Samtani et al. 2003).

The chief aim of this book is to describe how mobile multimedia messages are used by people in their ordinary daily activities. I focus on two main questions. First, what methods of expression do people use in designing multimedia messages? Second, how do people interact with each other through mobile multimedia? This book also has a more sociological aim, which is probed through a third question: what kinds of effects does mobile multimedia have on society? How does multimedia change mobile telephony? Does it make mobile telephony more practical, or does it simply become a visual, chatty channel fit for gossip but not for news? What kinds of social activities and organizations does it maintain, peer-to-peer networks only or also institutional ones?

These research questions are loosely motivated by what has become known as the social construction of technology (SCOT), perhaps best propounded by the Dutch sociologist and historian Wiebe E. Bijker (Bijker 1995; see also Hughes 1983; Latour 1987). In Bijker's opinion, any new technology is understood in many ways, particularly in its early stages where "interpretive flexibility" is at its highest. However, as time goes by, social forces try to impose more rigid perspectives on technological development, pushing towards more stable interpretation until in the final instance, only one of a few perspectives remain. Bijker calls this process "closure." In the context of mobile multimedia, it is clear that no closure has yet been achieved; rather, this technology is still in search of interpretation.

However, the central premise of this book is grounded in ethnomethodology: people come to define the nature of mobile multimedia technology in and through their ordinary actions. It is not technology as such, nor institutional forces like marketing, media, or company scenarios that define its fate. As people get new devices and new possibilities for communication, they may use industry and media frameworks as inspiration and, accordingly, come to construct mobile multimedia in the terms it was originally designed for. However, they may follow other courses as well. So, although the main ethos of this study follows SCOT as articulated by Bijker, I do not follow his research agenda in full. Rather, I focus on only one social force at work in reducing interpretive flexibility in technology: ordinary people using it for ordinary purposes.

Text Messages, Cameras, and Recorders as Technological Frames

Mobile multimedia phones combine the functions of several existing gadgets in one device. In designing and sending multimedia messages, you have to use at least one of these functions. In sharing a message, you have to send it through a procedure that is remarkably similar to sending a text message. You have to write a piece of text, select the recipient, and send the message. In addition, you can use two more functions. First, you can use the camera to capture photographs that are then inserted into the message. Secondly, you can use the recorder function in the phone to capture audio content—typically either talk or sounds—to be inserted into the message. These three functions both enable use and constrain it; they are key candidates for technological frames that people may use to define what kind of animal the multimedia phone is (cf. Bijker 1995: 191–197).

Are multimedia messages designed as text messages? After all, it is relatively easy to send a multimedia message instead of a text message, by simply adding a photograph or a piece of video to it. If this is the case, then multimedia messages function as enhanced text messages.

Beginning in around 1993, mobile phones became something more than just portable telephones: people could send text messages (SMS) consisting of first 20, then later 160 characters. Originally, the system was meant to function as pagers: you could send a short message to ask the other party to call (Kopomaa 2000: 60). However, by 1996 the SMS feature became widely available in phones, leading to something of a revolution in mobile telephony: SMS became the second main source of income for the telecommunications industry in addition to phone calls.

Text messaging has become successful because people use it for personal purposes rather than for services. In a survey of ten teenagers' messaging in Cambridgeshire, England, Grinter and Eldridge (2001) learned that roughly 15 percent of messages were sent to coordinate times and media for communicating face-to-face calls, or with instant messages. Roughly 5 percent of messages renegotiated these arrangements. About 20 percent of messages were gossip and chat about weekend plans, job interviews, and other news, but only about 10 percent were sent to family. Text messaging is quick and cheap, and with it one can avoid long conversations. It is also a convenient communication method when a phone call would be intrusive (for example, late at night) (Rivière 2002; also Nurmela et al. 2000: 13–15; Höflich and Rossler 2002: 93–95).

The first scholars who paid attention to text messages as a form of interaction were Kasesniemi (2003: 197–198, original in 2001), Taylor and Harper (2003), and Laursen (2005). Kasesniemi formulated two rules for proper SMS etiquette: first, a SMS message should be replied to with a text message; second, the message should be responded to as quickly as possible, generally within 30 minutes, or the recipient appears rude (Kasesniemi 2003: 197–198). Absent response is typically accounted for by problems in transmission or reception, by something said, or by something in the relationship (Laursen 2006: 53–63). The main exceptions to this rule are chain messages, messages received at night, and service messages like proverbs, horoscopes, and news that can go unanswered (Laursen 2006: 64–68). For example, in the following Danish example reported by Laursen (2005), Henrik expects a quick reply from Dorte, and when he does not get it, he "shouts" HELLO? "louder" (i.e., in caps) about an hour later. Laursen's proposal is that text messaging should be analyzed in terms of the formula A-B-A-B (and so forth), in which messages from A to B follow each other, always being tied to previous messages (see Message 1.2).

Message 1.2. (Laursen 2005: 58)

Henrik	09:11	HI dorte could you please tell grete that i'm ill?
Dorte	-	-
Henrik	10:18	HELLO?
Dorte	10:52	I have told it grete and ther's porno between anders and maja! It's really funny What r u doing? Hugzz.

Teenagers and young adults have been in the forefront in spreading text messages. Children start with games, transfer to text messages in early adolescence, then while in their late teens switch to voice. Mobile phones make it possible for them to maintain friendships despite their parents' interests (see the collection by Lorente 2002; Ling 2004: 145–147; Nurmela et al. 2002: 46–49). New cultural forms have emerged to mold the 160 characters for all these purposes. As Message 1.2 from Denmark already suggested, people created specific SMS languages to get the best out of 160 characters early on (Ling 2004: 162–163). For example, "want to talk" can be written "Wan2tlk?," which saves four characters (for example, see Grinter and Eldridge 2003; see also Kasesniemi 2003: 203–207; Mante-Meijer and Píres 2002: 56; Fortunati and Magnanelli 2002: 76–77; Lobet-Maris and Henin 2002: 112–113; Rivière 2002: 136–137).

Another key candidate for making sense of mobile multimedia comes
from the world of photography rather than mobile telephony. In what
ways do multimedia messages function as cameras rather than as text
messages? What sorts of uses can we expect to find if this is the case?

Perhaps the most sophisticated attempt to understand ordinary photography is *Kodak Culture* by Richard Chalfen (1987). In line with the
performative movement in folklore (Hymes 1964), he studies the "home
mode of imagery" as Kodak culture, which he defines in the following
terms:

> Kodak Culture will refer to whatever it is that one has to learn, know, *or* do in order
> to participate appropriately in what has been outlined as the home mode of commu-
> nication…. By studying Kodak culture, we want to learn how people have *organized*
> *themselves* socially to produce personalized versions of their own life experiences
> …. We want to consider how ordinary people have *organized their thinking* about
> personal pictures in order to understand certain pictorial messages and make mean-
> ingful interpretations in appropriate ways. We also want to learn how Kodak culture
> provides a structured and patterned way of looking at the world…we are examining
> how a "real world" gets transformed into a symbolic world. (Chalfen 1987: 10)

Finnish artist Seija Ulkuniemi (1998) has studied the contents of ordinary photographs, finding that the main contents of photographs are the
family and transitional rites (weddings, funerals, etc.); childhood homes
and first homes; symbols of social status (summer cottages, boats, firms,
etc.); nature; pets (especially children photograph pets); vacation and
tourist pictures (hotel windows, landscapes, buildings, relatives, picnics,
local life, beach life, trips, local inhabitants, group moments).

In everyday life, images interpret life for people by documenting it.
The documentary mode is possible given certain assumptions we make
about these images. For example, we believe that events in images have
taken place, and believe that we see these things just as they took place
when the original picture was taken (Ulkuniemi 1998: 126–127). Func-
tionally, however, images do not document our lives simply by creating
visual histories, validating, preserving, and encapsulating them, but also
by acting as *aide de memoire*, as memory banks, and as tools of cultural
membership. In photos, people do things right and grow into various
membership roles. For example, children learn the signs of success
and appropriate modes of kinship. Photography thus understood reifies
existing social bonds, documents changes in them, and thus orders the
mundane world (Chalfen 1987: 133–141). Photographs have usually been
interpreted as a tool for remembering (Halle 1994; Ulkuniemi 1998) and
building collective and individual identities.

As sociologist David Halle (1994) argues, photographs are the most important visual records in the home. The nature of these visual records, however, has changed over time. At first, photographs were similar to traditional portraits, romanticizing the family and its hierarchy. Family photographs began to change somewhat towards the end of the last century, however, and today people are embedded in the flow of events rather than made to stand out surrounded by status symbols. Instead of traditional formal pictures, photographs now show action, interaction, and people in informal dress. Simultaneously, pictures have moved from walls into albums and onto desks. For the modern American, photographs are a way of recording good memories, and no longer signs of power or status as in the earlier decades of the last century.

Of course, some ordinary photographic activities take more complex forms. According to Bourdieu's (1990) early French study, taking photographs and sharing them is not based on an all-encompassing aesthetic striving for beauty, but on ordinary social practices. For example, ordinary family portraits focus on important transitional rites like christenings, weddings, and funerals. The exceptions to this rule are photography clubs. In Bourdieu's data, middle-class photography clubs celebrate a picture's aesthetic values, whereas working-class clubs swear by technical mastery. Of course, for professionals, the camera is a more complicated instrument.[1]

Although photography itself has been much analyzed, audio in the context of photography has received scant attention by social scientists, with the exception of a small set of studies on portable stereos (see Hosokawa 1984; Bull 2000; Thibaud 2003). One design study has focused on how people link photographs with audio. David Frohlich (2004) gave several families an audiocamera to use on summer vacation. These "audiocameras" were a combination of an analog camera (Minolta AF 101R) and a dictaphone (Lanier P–155) unit glued together. Frohlich studied four types of sound: ambient sound, music, voiceovers, and storytelling attached to photographs. Music is usually entertaining and acts as a memory enhancer (Frohlich 2004: 105–107), while ambient sounds typically assist personal recollection by providing useful contextual information for reliving and for interpreting the original situation (in particular, Frohlich 2004: 76–77). In this study, audio had many uses. For example, ambient (i.e., natural) sounds—street noise, traffic sounds, music, background voices, birds singing, animals, rain, water, and in family scenes, sounds of people walking and laughing—add mood, atmosphere, and humor to photographs, and also compensate for bad photos (see also Frohlich and Tallyn 1999; Frohlich et al. 2002). In other words, a picture of Amsterdam's Damrak may be fun to watch if one can hear the voice of the street singer even though the picture is out of focus and difficult to interpret.

This brief review of the main technological constituents of mobile multimedia phones demonstrates that people have several sources to choose from when they design and send messages. If they use their experience from text messaging, multimedia becomes primarily an instrument for interaction. If they rely on their knowledge of photography, multimedia takes another track: people use their devices mainly for documenting ordinary things they want to remember later. The third possible preceding technology, audio recording, seems to build on photography. If the use of audio follows Frohlich's (2004) analysis, audio is integrated into multimedia mainly for emotional reasons and for explicating photographs. Chapter 2 evaluates these conjectures against the story told by the first studies of how real multimedia devices are used.

The Uses and Consequences of Mobile Phones

Recently, Kenneth Gergen (2007) analyzed how mobile telephony is transforming the political process and democracy. For him, the structure of political communication in Western societies has gone through a series of highly significant changes during the last fifty years. Between the government and the individual voter, there has always been a layer of face-to-face relationships in which people deliberate social issues and political issues. The fourth layer, a more recent addition, is mediated communication that was originally monological: the public was informed, but had only limited possibilities to participate in opinion formation in the media. However, with mobile phones, the nature of mediated communication changes. For example, in the Philippines, President Joseph Estrada reputedly fell victim to the power of SMS in 2001. With messages such as "Go 2EDSA, Wear blck," people organized a series of demonstrations at Epifanio de los Santos Avenue (EDSA), a major Manila thoroughfare, which led to the ousting of the president. The history of how Estrada lost his position was largely a story of massive demonstrations organized with mobile phone calls and text messages (Rheingold 2003a: 157–160; for a Hungarian case, see Dányi and Sükösd 2003). Although Pertierra et al. (2002: 101–124) have shown that other media environments were as important, with church and the president's opponents calling people for demonstrations in church services, TV, and radio, mobile phones no doubt played a part in the process.

We can call this picture optimistic. Mobile communication is an important constituent of what Kenneth Gergen calls "the proactive *Mittelbau*," opinion-formation and action that is rooted in the independent realities of civil society rather than in the opinions of political elites or the mass media.

However, the second picture Gergen paints is more somber. In this vision, civil society is being slowly replaced by small communication clusters, which increasingly take on the role previously played by face-to-face conversation in public venues. Political communication shifts from civil society to these "monadic clusters," as Gergen calls them. Instead of participating in society, people move through the day largely disengaged from those around them, turning instead to their friends when in trouble or in need of advice or encouragement. In these clusters, people focus on immediate life and micro-relationships at the cost of civic concerns. If they focus on issues relevant to democracy, they construct their opinions with their friends and acquaintances rather than in political parties or by participating in community decision making. People get detached from politics, which disrupts the dialogue necessary for a healthy democracy.

How does mobile multimedia fare in this scene? Koskinen (2007b) has reviewed its *Apparatgeist* in terms of Gergen's argument, concluding that the first sociological studies on mobile multimedia tend to point towards Gergen's second picture. For example, Scifo (2005) firmly situates camera phones and mobile multimedia in ordinary communication between friends and acquaintances, while Koskinen (2007a) has characterized mobile multimedia as machinery that produces banality: with it, people mainly capture and share ordinary things and events. In a darker tone, Rivière (2005) builds on French psychoanalysis, connecting ordinary uses of multimedia to the pleasure-seeking primary processes of the human psyche. For her, multimedia phones increase intimate communication, appealing to the sensations and spectacle:

> They increasingly use intimate play context, which have no rational purpose but rather aim at sensations, and in which the search for immediately shared pleasure is more and more visible. (Rivière 2005: 212)

If Rivière is right, multimedia in mobile phones upholds constant links between people who are remote from each other, thus reaffirming their relationships with contents that are meaningful only for them, but much less so for society at large (Licoppe 2004; Okabe and Ito 2006; Ling 2006).

A possible exception to this conclusion may be what has come to be known as "moblogs" (see Rheingold 2003b; Ito 2004). People can share images and other multimedia content they have captured—or received—on their multimedia phones not just by showing them on the screen, or by sending them to another phone. They can also put their images on the World Wide Web; software in newer phones even makes it fairly easy to create a Web site with the phone. If one sends text to these sites to augment images, a photo album turns into a "moblog," a Web-based diary-like site from which readers can follow the writer's life and opinions on a constant basis. However, this practice seems to be unusual even in Japan, where a moblog culture first took off around 2002. According to a government survey reported by Okada, only 0.6 percent of Webphone (mobile phones with access to the Internet) owners had created a Web site. More prevalent uses (>30 percent of users had tried at least once during the past year) were e-mail, music file downloads, image downloads, and visits to games/fortune telling sites (Okada 2005: 49). In terms of the journalistic uses of moblogs, they seem to center around sharing newsworthy events in one's personal life and "stalking" celebrities with cam phone pictures rather than "serious" journalism. Although Ito (2004) tells about the "*Sha-mail* Diary Confederation" (*sha-mail* refers to a popular handset) that had twenty-nine writers sharing their diaries of *sha-mail* photos in 2004, this seems to be a rare occurrence. The global situation today does not change this picture. In a recent study of moglogs, Döring and Gundolf (2005) observed that although by 2004 there were already hundreds of thousands of moblogs globally, only few were active after the first week.

However, pictures and video captured with mobile devices do occasionally enter the mass media, as in the case of the bombings in the London underground in the summer of 2004 when the first footage from actual sites of bombings was shot by tourists and Londoners with camera phones. The first Finnish case took place in the summer of 2002, when an electronics shop owner managed to take pictures of a bank robbery in the town of Turku with his camera phone. These pictures were published in tabloids. The global breakthrough of camera phones to media took place in the aftermath of the Asian *tsunami* in December 2004 and al-Qaeda's terrorist attack in London underground in summer 2005. Camera phone pictures from "tube" tunnels even appeared on the front pages of the *New York Times* and the *Washington Post* (Dunleavy 2005). No statistics exist, but we can safely assume that moblogging has a long way to go before it is as popular as the practice of building Home Pages and "weblogs" on the Web.

Thus, with the possible exceptions of moblogging in Japan and citizen journalism, a safe guess is that moblogs are not a particularly popular form of sharing mobile multimedia content. A good deal of sharing takes place on the screen, or through multimedia messaging services rather than through the Web. A small selection of particularly newsworthy or personally significant messages appears on the Web, but the selection is wider on phones. Furthermore, moblogs are subject to a different set of social processes—for example, journalistic ethics—than mobile imaging in phones. It is likely that mobile multimedia cannot be taken as a special case of the Web, or something that is going to converge with it, as its use is organized differently.

Definitions

A few restrictions must be kept in mind when reading this book. First, the focus is consistently on ordinary people, not on occupational or professional uses (see Ling and Julsrud 2005). Professions inevitably develop methods that differ from ordinary uses for any technology to support their work. Secondly, the focus is on actual messages rather than attitudes, opinions, or what people say about use (see Kindberg et al. 2004; Okabe and Ito 2006). Chapter 14 explains the data in detail, but let me say here that it consists of a mass of actual messages sent in Helsinki and other parts of Southern Finland between 1999 and 2002. Third, since these data comes from the early days of mobile multimedia, the focus is on still images and sound files sent with phones rather than video (see Kasesniemi et al. 2003). Fourth, I focus on personal and social messaging rather than what can be called mobile mass media, including mobile TV and mobile movies (see Ok 2005; Koskinen 2007b).

It is also important to keep in mind that this book is based on what can be called the first generation of mobile multimedia phones. These phones had an in-built camera, and some of them made it possible for people to capture and send sound files as well. With a few phones, it was also possible to construct simple animations. Compared to the newest phones, these devices were technologically simple. In particular, the quality of cameras and recording equipment was far worse than in today's phones. Partly for this reason, this study focuses on how people communicate with each other, since the methods used in communication do not age as fast as technology.

The book is mainly based on European and, to a small extent, Japanese experience chiefly because there is little data on mobile multimedia in North America today. For this reason, it would be risky to generalize conclusions about visual culture in mobile multimedia, for example, since European visual culture obviously differs from American. However, since the focus is on methods of action, it is likely that this analysis gives an idea of what happens in other cultures as well. Finally, with a few exceptions, the book builds on research in which either a large number of people have been studied, or in which small groups have been followed for a long time. There is no lack of technological research on mobile multimedia, but typical user research in technological research normally consists of only a few users (often technology or psychology students) observed for a very short time. This canon works in practical usability work in industry (see Nielsen 1994), but is theoretically too poor for social science. For the same reason, the book does not analyze mobile multimedia art. There have been several photographic exhibitions using camera phones all over the world ranging from Norway and Finland to California, and even photographic books have been published (Banks et al. 2002).

In conceptual terms, this book will consistently speak about people instead of "users," a term that is used in technological and business literature, but suggests some undesirable connotations. In essence, it focuses too much on human-device interaction, and less on people (see Bannon 1991), which is the main reason for preferring the richer, lay notion of "people."

It is important to understand one feature of the nature of this analysis. The philosopher Karl Popper (1963) made a distinction between the context of discovery and the context of justification. The latter means science, which starts from a well-tested, accumulated body of theoretical statements and concepts. Clearly, studies in mobile multimedia are not in such a state today. Rather, they work in the context of discovery, in which it is still more important to articulate observations and interpret them theoretically for future testing. I have attempted to do just that: to make a series of observations, and elaborate them by relating them to some ideas in classic ethnomethodology. It remains the task of future studies to point out problems and gaps in the analysis presented herein.

Many messages are used to illustrate the book's arguments. The reader ought to keep in mind that these are original images captured with the first generation of camera phones, so consequently the image quality is typically low.

The Structure of the Book

The structure of the book is based on the research questions outlined above. The book is divided into four parts. Part I, "Introduction and Theoretical Perspectives," ties the book to existing literature, and introduces the book's theoretical perspective. Chapter 2 asks what mobile multimedia does to mobile telephony, how it changes technology that has already redefined our ways of interacting and relating to the world and other people. Chapter 3 outlines the theoretical perspective that has guided empirical work, arguing that we need an ethnomethodological perspective when doing empirical analysis. The Chapter ends with a critical look at existing literature on mobile multimedia. The criticism is based on the arguments of early ethnomethodology, which claim that social science needs to study actual use rather than use it as an unproblematic resource for analysis.

Part II, "Design Elements of Mobile Multimedia," focuses on the first research question, the methods of expression used by people in designing multimedia messages. Chapter 4 focuses on cultural forms that people use to construct multimedia messages. For example, there are many types of postcard-like messages in multimedia data, ranging from travel and tourist photographs to greetings, good night wishes, and love letters. In Chapter 5, the focus is on how people use the audiocapture function built into multimedia phones. It introduces the notions of "foreground" and "ambient" sound, and then analyzes how these function in messages. For instance, does the foreground function as a "voice mail," or is it simply used for greetings? What does ambient street noise communicate? How does sound function in the sequence of messages, and how do recipients interpret sounds? The conclusion discusses how sound augments visual multimedia. Chapter 6 takes a close look at the uses of the body in mobile multimedia. Faces and other bodily parts are ubiquitous in multimedia messages, and are used in several ways in communication. This Chapter shows how the body appears as an expressive instrument in multimedia messages.

Part III, "Mobile Multimedia as Interaction," focuses on the second research question, how people interact with each other with this technology. It makes the case for studying multimedia as a naturally occurring activity. Chapter 7 looks at how people make messages interesting for the recipient, and how they try to secure a response. In essence, this Chapter shows how people are held accountable for communicating only interesting things. What distinguishes mobile multimedia from other forms of traditional media is its interactivity. While some messages are simply received and not responded to, this is not always the case. Chapter 8 studies the main types of recipient activities following Erving Goffman's (1981) useful distinction between replies and responses. Chapter 9 examines how people try to stop messaging. There are several reasons for such attempts: for instance, previous messages may be too banal, teases may go overboard, or messages may be too obscene. This Chapter focuses on methods used in trying to close messages, and what can be called "relational work in closings": there are always elements that soften the closing. It is this interactivity that makes mobile multimedia different from such traditional media forms as photographs and postcards.

The three chapters of Part IV, "Mobile Multimedia in Society," attempt to answer the third research question, probing the consequences of mobile multimedia. Chapter 10 shifts attention to society at large, that is, how institutions like politics and the economy are occasioned in mobile multimedia. For example, can mobile multimedia sensitize people to inequalities in society? Or is society only a fleeting phenomenon of passing interest on the small screen of the mobile phone? Chapter 11 examines multimedia messaging in "strong" relationships—friends, acquaintances, couples—and focuses on one "latent function" (Merton 1968) of multimedia messaging, its ability to update social information. For instance, one section of the Chapter studies how people introduce new people in multimedia messages, and how these introductions lead to inquiries concerning these people. Finally, Chapter 12 focuses on the question of whether people are creating new uses for mobile multimedia. Are people creative adapters of new multimedia, or is its adoption a culturally driven process? This Chapter rephrases this issue by focusing on how people "discover" uses for their phones. The Chapter closes with a discussion of the pros and cons of the culturalist and the creative arguments, and evaluates them from a more action-focused standpoint.

Chapter 13 begins by reinstating the basic point of this book: mobile multimedia is a technology for communication and interaction. The next section briefly reviews existing theoretical attempts to study mobile multimedia and contrasts them with the perspective developed in this book. The third section is a response to Kenneth Gergen's (2006) recent analysis of how mobile telephony functions in democracy. As we have seen, Gergen paints a picture of technology that is disruptive of civil society but may simultaneously empower it. The final section maintains that it is important to understand mundane uses of technology by studying how it is actually used. Finally, Chapter 14 describes the data and methods, evaluating their strengths and weaknesses. It also deals with ethical principles followed in these studies.

Note

1. It should be kept in mind that Bourdieu's views of everyday aesthetics are dated and are based on assumptions about the nature of society as it existed in France in the 1950s and 1960s. For example, he assumes that upper-class taste defines true reality, and is filtered down gradually to the less well-off. This assumption has become all the more difficult to uphold in the new millennium.

2

Multimedia in Mobile Telephony

With the introduction of cameras in phones, people got access to a wide array of new expressive possibilities that were not previously at their disposal. In contrast to industry scenarios that gave mobile multimedia a central place in the future of mobile telephony, this Chapter shows that something different was happening in ordinary society. Even as business analysts, marketing departments of phone manufacturers, and governments were playing technological and financial games on mobile multimedia, building scenarios of markets-to-come, others were busy trying to figure out what features people would like to have in their phones in the future.

The first studies on how people use mobile multimedia focused on image capture and sharing, and were published around 2000. Before these studies, the only relevant research was based on early attempts to introduce video telephony (Schnaars and Wymbs 2004) and studies on videoconferencing (see Heath and Luff 2000). This comparison helped to point out several problems in visual communication—for instance, what happens when people move away from the camera or use subtle visual cues that are impossible to see on screen—but the latter comparison in particular was riddled with problems. Not only was the technology itself totally different, but also the context of use of videoconferencing equipment was too different from mobile technology to provide useful understanding. Thus, the first design studies took another option, aiming instead at exploring technical facets and also various modes of expression (cf. Mäkelä et al. 2000). These modes were photographs, audio, and text. A still more realistic research agenda arose in 2002, when the first mobile multimedia phones came to the European and the North American markets. This Chapter turns to the first empirical studies, focusing on how people use multimedia phones, in order to clarify the methods of expression people use in designing multimedia messages and how they interact with each other through mobile multimedia.

Kodak Culture on the Phone

In one of the first studies on how camera phones have been used, Okabe and Ito (2004) note that unlike traditional cameras, the camera phone is becoming practically ubiquitous in Japan. It follows people everywhere, making new kinds of visual and personal awareness possible. It alerts people to see visually interesting things as potentially recordable and communicable. In a Japanese survey probing the question of what people take most pictures of, the most prevalent response was "things that they happened upon that were interesting" (42.4 percent), followed by pictures of family members (39.5 percent), friends (36.6 percent), self (26.4 percent), pets (23.7 percent), and from travels (21.5 percent) (Okabe and Ito 2004), much as in ordinary snapshot photography (Chalfen 1987; Koskinen et al. 2002: 21–26).

Figure 2.1 is from a British and American study. Kindberg et al. (2004) classified multimedia messages sent by nineteen Britons (nine teenagers, ten adults) and fifteen Americans (four and eleven, respectively, from the San Francisco Bay Area), recruited from the researchers' own organizations and their communities. Each participant was interviewed twice. In both interviews, people showed images from their phone to researchers, who queried about the image, its capture, and the intentions behind it. They also asked for details on the uses of these images and on what the interviewees would have wanted to do with them. Out of 349 messages analyzed, 82 percent were affective in nature. German figures corroborate this analysis (Döring et al. 2005).

Figure 2.1
The Contents of Pictures in Multimedia Messages

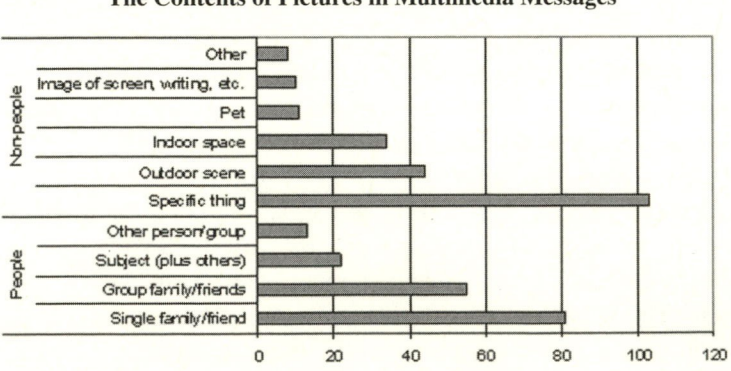

(Kindberg et al. 2004)

Perhaps the best way to interpret these results is by comparing them to Chalfen's (1987) *Kodak culture* thesis. Although Chalfen rightly notes that switching from more rigid early-century photographic practices to the more informal Kodak culture profoundly changed photography, it looks like with mobile multimedia phones, people capture things in an even less planned way than with, say, Polaroid cameras. A good deal of the Kodak culture images still focus on family rituals, possessions, and travels. Images captured with camera phones open even less significant aspects of life to visual attention. Things are captured because they are worth remembering later, but many images seem to be captured just on a whim, designed to provide fun or information only for a moment. In Kodak culture on the phone, photographs are barely more than a spur of the moment, designed for no other purpose than to have fun for a few seconds before being discarded.

Capture and See, Capture and Send: Functions of Multimedia Messages

As Kindberg et al. (2004) have pointed out, a good deal of mobile multimedia use is for immediate seeing rather than for sending. That is, people use camera phones to capture images for seeing on the phone rather than for sending. Pictures in the phone form a photographic archive of memories, a mobile archive, which is "always within easy reach...when feeling nostalgic, or just to pass an interstitial moment in one's daily routine" (Scifo 2005: 365–366). Following Smith and Watson (1996), Cooley takes this observation one step further by talking about an "autobiographical impulse," defined as "the act of self-evidencing attributable to mobile imaging produced images which comprise an ever-expanding visual *statistical* archive." As she notes, the emphasis is no longer placed "on the images themselves...imaging itself is what matters" (Cooley 2005). According to Cooley, pictures in one's phone gradually build up an "autobiometrical" apparatus that makes it possible for people to study their life as it evolves.

In contrast to these mainly private uses, some images are shared with friends on the screen. For example, in their 2000-2001 study of mobile multimedia, Koskinen and his colleagues noted this social aspect of digital images:

> When the result is immediately visible, it is easier for photographers to hone their skills. Due to the memory card in the camera, the user also always carries along a load of photographs which can be shown to friends. The pictures do not need to be developed, nor, necessarily, even sent to others. The interviewees appreciated this

feature of being able to view pictures on the camera, and considered it a vehicle of sociability. For example, Minna said that the members of the female group had the habit that whenever they met, they immediately "viewed all the pictures the others had in their cameras." (Koskinen et al. 2002: 138)

However, people also share images with other people over the wireless network. What kinds of images do they share and why? According to Okabe and Ito, using a camera typically requires planning: people think ahead about what is important and memorable enough for photographing. People capture ceremonies (like weddings) and picturesque places (typically, when vacationing abroad). In contrast, mobile multimedia follows people everywhere, and renders picture-worthy even the less notable aspects of everyday life (Okabe and Ito 2004). Thus, multimedia phones may not radically change the objects in pictures, but they change the selection of shootables: "cam phones are also being used to capture and share what people consider more noteworthy events that others might be interested in" (Okabe 2004). Camera phone images lack the reflection and planning typical of images taken with traditional camera technology. Compared to earlier forms of ordinary photography—for example, formal portraits, family rituals—existing evidence suggests that mobile multimedia primarily follows in the footsteps of the Kodak culture (Chalfen 1987).

In a more recent analysis of Japanese data, Okabe and Ito (2006) analyzed practices of camera phone photography. They categorize these uses into three main classes. First, some pictures are not meant to be sent, but are taken for personal visual archiving. They consist of scenes and viewpoints on everyday life. Second, among friends, most messaging consists of peer-to-peer news and reporting of ordinary events, things, and activities. Third, couples capture and send images of ordinary things and events just to show that the sender is thinking of the other party. Okabe and Ito call this practice "intimate visual co-presence."

Ito (2005) offers a more general symbolic interpretation of the last of these findings. Koskinen (2005a) has noted that people often share pictures that are not really interesting by making them interesting, for example, by explaining why a sunrise is beautiful enough to be worth sending. Still, underlying this work is an assumption that people share meaningful, significant events. However, as Ito has noted, this does not seem to hold for couples in an intimate relationship. Instead, they tend to share images of ordinary things to maintain "visual co-presence." These messages are not designed to communicate images, but to show the recipient that he or she is in the sender's mind—and to get the recipient to think about him or her for a moment. The message is a symbol designed to maintain and refresh the relationship (see also Scifo 2005).

Of course, people use multimedia phones for several "instrumental" purposes, too. Scifo (2005) distinguishes three such uses. First, performative messages are used to micro-coordinate group activities. For instance, people send images of places to show where they want the recipient to go. Second, some messages are plainly informative—like pictures of road accidents. Third, problem-solving messages are sent in order to reduce time and cost and to solve emergencies. These messages may consist of "the reproduction of maths formulas or of book pages so as to stealthily use them while taking a written examination" (Scifo 2005).

Finally, people sometimes share images just for fun. Snapping pictures during moments of fun and games among friends may not be particularly interesting, but still the pictures are worth sending for sharing fun (Scifo 2005: 366). Extrapolating from this observation, Battarbee (2004; Battarbee and Koskinen 2004) has coined the term "co-experience," to help us make sense of the social aspects of experience. Her analysis shifts the locus of analysis from the individual to the social level: when people experience something significant enough to capture, they bring it to the attention of other people, thus sharing that experience. Often the original experience is social at the outset: it is the very fact that something takes place in the company of others that makes it into an experience. Through their responses, others reinterpret that experience, shaping the way in which it proceeds. This joint work often takes place either before or long after the actual experience. In this analysis, "experience" does not have to be fleeting, or even actual: it can be the result of years of symbolic work.

How Actual Messages are Designed and Shared

A small set of studies has collected actual messages sent by people to study use instead of reconstructing usage from interviews. Ling and Julsrud (2005) focus on the "genres" of multimedia messaging. They studied MMS in small work groups with dense internal networks in Norway. Groups were composed of mobile salespersons for a soft drink company, real estate salespersons, and carpenters. Each group was given an access to MMS for six months. Ling and Julsrud learned that the main genres were documentation of work-related objects, visualization of details and project status; snapshots (developing camaraderie); postcards and greetings; and chain messages (standardized messages, usually downloaded from Web sites). Soft drink salespersons used MMS most, followed by carpenters. These groups used MMS for all of the above-mentioned purposes. Real estate salespersons used the technology only for postcards, greetings, and snapshots. Carpenters also used MMS for "clarification": taking and sending pictures of problems at work to get advice from colleagues. With slightly different classifications, similar views have been put forth by Okabe (2005) and Jacucci et al. (2006).

In contrast to the domestication and the genre arguments, two bodies of research direct attention to how people interact with each other with multimedia messages. The gift exchange model, proposed by several writers (Johnsen 2000, 2003; Licoppe and Heurtin 2001; Taylor and Harper 2002; Kasesniemi 2003; Harper 2003), can be readily extended to analyze multimedia messages. The following example is again from the writer's archives. He had visited friends to see their newborn baby. He took a picture of the baby, and sent it to another friend. She responded with the following message, which not only makes evident her delight, but also rewards him with another child-related photograph (Message 2.1). The point is that when a person sends a message, it creates an obligation to respond either with a thank you note, or with a "counter-gift." If no response follows, then the recipient remains in debt, and may even be reproached for this gaffe.

Message 2.1
Easter Bunnies

What an adorable baby! In exchange you get an Easter Bunny postcard.

Useful as the gift analogy is, it is restricted in scope. In contrast, Koskinen and his colleagues have studied mobile multimedia as interaction from a situated perspective (Koskinen et al. 2002; Koskinen and Kurvinen 2002; Battarbee 2004). In *Mobile Image*, they gave a Nokia Communicator, an advanced PDA-like phone and a Casio camera to four groups of five people for approximately two months each. People could beam photographs from the camera to the phone via an infrared link, and send them as an attachment in mobile e-mails. In this study, photographing became even more mundane and ad hoc than early design studies (see Mäkelä et al. 2000). Most images were construed as group poses, postcards, and so forth. More interestingly, images became interactive: people used the system not only for sending images, but also for commenting on them with text and, sometimes, images. In contrast to classifying messages into genres, this analysis shifts focus to the actual elements used in designing messages, and the ways in which recipients respond to them. (For a similar approach to text messages, see Laursen 2005).

However, the equipment of *Mobile Image* was too slow for viewing images "on the fly": it took well over a minute from taking a picture to sending it, and another minute to download it from mail. Not surprisingly, when Koskinen and his colleagues studied messaging with actual multimedia phones in which the process takes only a few seconds, they found and described more intricate forms of interaction (Koskinen 2003, 2005a). For example, Kurvinen (2002) showed how people share not only serious emotions—such as love—with multimedia, but also flimsy ones, such as apathy following a party. In another paper, Kurvinen focused on how people tease each other with pictures (Kurvinen 2002, 2003; also Battarbee and Koskinen 2004). Koskinen (2005a) showed how people make photographs mutually intelligible by asking questions about their fuzzy details. In this analysis, photographs and other multimedia elements are something people use in interaction for practical purposes. In this sense, the multimedia elements are not extraneous or technology-driven, separate from human intention.

Discussion

In only fifteen years, mobile telephony has evolved from a business tool into a global industry. With mobile phones, text messaging, and the mobile Internet, people have acquired new ways of experiencing and sharing things in their lives, as well as interacting with the marketplace.

With good reason, mobile telephony has been called a mind-altering and society-altering technology (Katz and Aakhus 2002: 2–3). But does this new mobile multimedia add anything new to our picture of mobile telephony and text messaging? In answering this question, it is advisable to start with a few caveats. For one, at the end of 2005 there was still no coordinated research basis, and theoretical and methodological discussion had barely started. Also, much like studies on mobile telephony more generally, the best studies are case studies of fairly small groups in culturally uniform settings. Thus, any sweeping generalizations have to be treated with caution.

However, a few outlines are possible. Existing literature suggests that the "home base" of mobile multimedia is mutual entertainment rather than purposive communication or commercial services (for example, Mäkelä et al. 2000; Ling and Julsrud 2005; Koskinen et al. 2002; Okabe and Ito 2004; Scifo 2005). Mobile multimedia is a personal technology rather than mass media; it functions much as mobile phones and text messages, not as the Internet, which has given rise to major service industries. Also, a good amount of mobile multimedia messages are never sent; rather, the phone functions as a portable memory for photographs and sounds. Perhaps more than anything else, mobile multimedia adds emotional content and fun to small groups rather than opens them up to wider society. The word "telecocooning" may describe it best (see Habuchi 2005: 178–179; comp. to Koskinen et al. 2002; Scifo 2005). Multimedia technology links people to their friendship networks, where it primarily nourishes sentimental bonds, following the formulation of the Italian sociologist Barbara Scifo (2005).

Existing research is suggestive rather than conclusive on matters relating to how actual messages are designed and how they are used in action. With the main exception of work done by Koskinen and his colleagues (Koskinen et al. 2002; Kurvinen 2003; Battarbee 2004), there are few studies of how actual messages are constructed, and how they are responded to by recipients. Since research has focused mainly on photography, it has tended to stress having fun and preserving memories rather than, say, more practical or unconstructive uses. Thus, although van House and Davis (2005) distinguish three main classes of uses for multimedia phones, most work has concentrated on the first of these functions. As van House and Davis note, phones are first of all *memory-capture devices*. Camera phones are used to capture images of memory-worthy events, but unlike other kinds of cameras, they are also used to capture mundane images. Secondly, they are used as *communicative devices*. Many images are captured specifically for communicative use, whether from the phone or from a Web site. Third, they are *expressive devices*. They are used to capture expressive images, including art and humor. With these means, messages express the photographer's sensibility and view of the world.

The theoretical argument of this book tries to correct this situation. So far, people have mainly been studying memory-capture, but we also need to study how people actually express themselves and communicate with other people through their phones. Initial evidence suggests that mobile multimedia is an interactive technology rather than a mass media or a distribution channel for services. People interact with mobile multimedia by sending and replying to messages. However, with the exception of the studies by Koskinen and his colleagues (for example, Koskinen et al. 2002; Koskinen 2005a,b) and Kurvinen (2002, 2003), the element missing from existing studies is real messages in action: we lack descriptions of *how* people *do* things with multimedia devices and multimedia messages. To understand properly what people do with mobile multimedia, we need to recover the actual activity and make it the topic of analysis rather than just a resource (Zimmerman and Pollner 1970). This task begins in Chapter 3 and continues throughout the rest of the book.

3

Mobile Multimedia in Action

*In doing sociology...every reference to the "real world..." is a reference to the
organized activities of everyday life. Thereby, in contrast to certain versions of Durkheim that teach that the objective reality of social facts is
sociology's fundamental principle, the lesson is taken instead...that the
objective reality of social facts as an ongoing accomplishment of the con-
certed activities of daily life...is a fundamental phenomenon.*

--Garfinkel 1967: vii

In this quote, Harold Garfinkel outlines the basic policy of ethnomethodology. The central recommendation of this alternative to traditional
sociology is that the "activities whereby members produce and manage
settings of organized everyday affairs are identical with members' procedures for making those settings accountable" (Garfinkel 1967: 1). In
plain English, this means that we need to study how people do things
instead of explaining their actions by, say, gender, personality, or reciprocal obligations posed by gifts.

From this perspective, practical human activity is an endless, ongoing,
and contingent accomplishment. In doing things, people rely on an im-
mense set of "ethnomethods," ordinary people's ordinary methods (see
Garfinkel 1967: 31; Garfinkel 1975),[1] such as questions and answers
(Schegloff and Sacks 1973) and postcards (Tainio 1999). People observe
ongoing actions with these same methods, and hold others accountable
for relying on them. More is at stake than mere convenience: if people's
sense of order is shattered by action that does not follow these methods,
their trust in their ability to be competent, rational, and predictable is also
shattered. They may then get bewildered or angry, and may demand an
explanation or an apology (Garfinkel 1967: 41–65). For example, a question that goes unanswered normally elicits a repeat question or a demand
for an explanation of why the person is being rude unless circumstances
like noise account for the absence of the reply (see Schegloff and Sacks

1973; Heritage 1989: 246–247; Sacks 1995, II: 35–37). The analyst's task is to describe these mundane practices.

Good examples of how such description takes place come from ethnomethodological studies of how "representations" cannot be separated from action. Any representation—painting, image, scientific graph, video, map, and so forth—organizes the viewer's perceptual field, forming a gestalt contexture (Gurwitsch 1964). However, seeing is a practical, methodic activity rather than something organized by the representation only (see Ochs et al. 1994: 152). For example, Heath et al. (2002a) studied Jason Cleverly's interactive art piece, *Deus Oculi*, which consisted of a Renaissance scene and two false mirrors that were in fact cameras. People who were looking into the mirrors appeared in the painting, which had two faces behind a little door. People discovered the "functionalities of the piece...largely in and through interaction with others, both people accompanying other people and others who happen to be in the same place" (Heath et al. 2002a: 18).

Ethnomethodological studies on representations show that seeing is a bodily and often a social activity. People routinely point at things on screens with their fingers and other pointing devices, thus highlighting what is important in them (see Heath and Luff 2000: 168–175; see Goodwin 1995: 258; vom Lehn et al. 2001: 196–198; Heath and Luff 2000: 165–168; Goodwin 1994: 622–624). Some of these practices are institutionalized into coding schemes and theoretical contracts, as in police work and airport controllers' work (see Goodwin 1994; Goodwin and Goodwin 1996: 77–79). Just as often, however, there is no such professional basis, as when people browse through their photo albums (Frohlich et al. 2002; Chalfen 1987). The central message of these studies is that when analyzing representations of any kind, we need to study them as a pair in which representations and human activities are inseparable (see Garfinkel 1996).

Text, Image, and Sound:
Expression in Mobile Multimedia Messages

Mobile multimedia provides people with the technical means to capture and share things they come up with in their lives. In doing so, they may utilize text, talk, sounds, images—and sometimes video. As Okabe and Ito (2004) note, with mobile multimedia phones, people become amateur photojournalists of sorts. In comparison to traditional cameras, camera phones capture "the more fleeting and unexpected moments of surprise, beauty and adoration in the everyday." They also invite sharing immediate, ad hoc and ongoing observations. In Okabe and Ito's words, ordinary things become the site of potential news and visual archiving, much as with digital cameras more generally (see also Koskinen et al. 2002: 138).

Following Garfinkel (1967) and ethnomethodological studies on representations, Koskinen et al. (2002) argue that although any elements of mobile multimedia can be understood in several ways, in actual messages these elements define each other in a reflexive fashion.

To see how individual messages are designed from elements that as such can be interpreted in many ways, let us turn to Message 3.1, sent by Anna from a stormy sea to her friends. This message can be understood in many ways if we look at its individual elements only. Such interpretation, however, would be misleading in many cases. For example, audio and text both talk about the wonderful holiday weather, while in the photograph, there is a person dressed in clothes that bespeak less than perfect holiday weather. In contrast, taken as a whole, the message is obviously humorous, possibly making a sarcastic comment on the storm at sea. It is only by looking at all details in the message in their specific constellation that we understand its design; any attempt to derive its meaning from individual multimedia elements would lead us astray.

Message 3.1
Greetings from the Sea

True holiday weather!
Audio: Anna Hi Timo! Greetings from sunny Jussarö! We're coming with Lena slowly towards Porkkala. As you see from the picture, the weather is really good.

Of course, the ways in which people construe messages goes beyond those relatively simple means implied in the preceding analysis. Multimedia devices provide more than a means for capturing things in the environment: they also provide the means to exploit many kinds of orderly, conventional means of expression. These means range from Hollywood-style narratives to facial expressions and age-old gestures. Ordinary life and its orderly features bombard people with resources that can be exploited in action, and many others can easily be staged.

One class of such means of expression consists of what can be called traditional media formats. In the "Postcard from Greece" in Chapter 1, my friend sent me a photograph of sunny skies and a windmill, asked me to imagine an old beach café keeper who lives in the mill, and described how his family is relaxing in this scene. Simultaneously, the text reduced prominent elements in the photograph—like the windmill—to barely more than a scenic background for holiday activities. With such assistance, I knew what he wanted me to see in the photograph. As this example shows, people may use traditional media formats to organize their observations and reflections into meaningful messages.

Message 3.1 also shows that just like traditional media formats, sound offers multiple means of expression in the mobile domain. People sometimes add sound to explain messages and to create atmosphere and aid memory. As Frohlich and Tallyn learned in a study on audio in photography, sound adds to mood, atmosphere and humor, revives bad photos, and acts as "extra triggers for people's memory of the events being recorded" (Frohlich and Tallyn 1999: 297). In addition to talk and ambient sounds (see Koskinen 2005c), people may add music and stories to messages to assist remembering and understanding (Frohlich 2004). However, sometimes photographs and video explain text and audio: it is important not to give priority to any media element on a theoretical basis without examining individual messages (Frohlich 2004; Koskinen 2005c).

Finally, Message 3.1 uses still another communicative resource available to multimedia users, the body. In this message, the body and clothing become the main cue for making sense of the message as a sarcastic commentary on stormy and cold vacation weather. Koskinen (2005a) has analyzed a case in which four women sent a photograph of themselves to Markku, a young man, asking him to pay attention to Patsy's open cleavage. Markku responded by sending a picture in which he held his hand in front of his eyes as if he was seeing something so terrible that he had to turn his head away. In text, he asked the women to "cover Patsy's cleavage with a safety pin or something" (see Messages 6.2–6.3). Such gestures range from good night kisses to cheers with a glass of sparkling wine and grinning faces (Battarbee 2003; Kurvinen 2003). In a similar manner, hearing-impaired people can use sign language through short video clips (Kasesniemi et al. 2003).

Mobile multimedia, then, goes beyond seeing things and responding to them as such. Consequently, it would be misleading to study it merely as an extension of camera technology, mobile telephony, or text messaging. Instead, it is better to study it as a multi-sensory toolbox that makes it possible for people to seize ordinary means of expression for the purposes of interaction.

Mobile Multimedia as Interaction

Often, a multimedia message is a starting point for interaction only. Recipients do several kinds of things when they receive mobile multimedia messages. Of course, they have to make sense of messages. However, recipient activities go far beyond mere interpretation. For instance, they routinely respond to greetings and "thank you" notes with return greetings and "you're welcome" messages. Also, they make inquiries about events, objects, and people with which they are not familiar. Some things in messages may also be unidentifiable because the intention behind an image is unclear (Koskinen et al. 2002: Ch. 6; Frohlich 2004; Koskinen 2005a). For example, Frohlich et al (2002: 170–172) have shown how two people, Simon and Tracy, identify objects and spaces in Tracy's photo album.

What recipients do largely depends on what the sender has done. Often messages make a reply possible, but do not require one. Postcards are an obvious example: I did not answer the "Postcard from Greece," and was not reprimanded for that. Often messages are curious or funny enough to call forth a response: even though nothing as such tells the recipient what to do, the message clearly has a point that requires a response. For example, sarcastic and exaggerated messages call forth teases as a natural reply (Atkinson and Drew 1979; Kurvinen 2003).

However, sometimes senders instruct the recipient more significantly with what this book calls "response instructions." People almost always respond to messages that contain response instructions. For example, in Message 3.2, Tom sends greetings to Ann Marie, who replies 17 minutes later with a return greeting, which shows Tom two things: that Anna had received the message, and that she had understood it properly (see Message 3.3).

Message 3.2
Greetings

July 2 2002 19:16 Tom to Ann Marie
Greetings.

Message 3.3
Return Greeting

July 2 2002 19:33 Ann Marie to Tom
Greetings back to you! Also from mom!

These recipient acts are coherent with expectations elicited in earlier messages. Following Goffman (1981: 35), they will be called "replies," and distinguished from "responses." Responses are messages in which the recipient abstracts from the earlier message and responds to it in a creative fashion. An example of a response is a joke about the dialect in a question about time and a request for a more specific question.

Responses can be creative up to being unconventional. Building on Gurwitsch (1964: esp. 135-136, 217), I will reserve the term "gestalt modification" for them. Typically, these modifications are done by extracting one part of the earlier message and by embedding that part into another contexture that modifies its meaning radically.

Koskinen et al. (2002: 34–35) describe a case in which one participant sent a postcard-like image of an upscale shopping street in downtown Helsinki (Message 3.4). The response was anything but expected. One recipient added a huge green face of a colleague into the horizon, and shook the image digitally so that it looked like the camera had been moving up and down while the photograph was being taken. The text explained the addition: the Godzilla-size creature in the horizon was "The Giant Green Sociologist" who threatened the city (Message 3.5). Nothing in the original image could anticipate such a response, devised as a tease to the colleague, who liked self-portraits of his face. The referents of the original photograph remained, but they took place in a radically new context of interpretation.

In turn, any response provides the opportunity for another response. For example, a tease not only formulates the preceding message as somehow laughable, but also provides the teased person with an opportunity to laugh along with the teaser, to demand an apology, or to turn teasing into an exchange of insults. Depending on this action, the teaser gets further opportunities to act. In this way, any response is "doubly contextual," a contribution to an ongoing activity while simultaneously a starting point for the next action (Heritage 1989: 242). It is this interplay of messages and responses that gives mobile multimedia its characteristic social organization. The social organization of mobile multimedia is by and large "local," organized more on a message-by-message basis rather than by structural issues such as occupational forms of reasoning or behaving (see Wilson 1991; Ling and Julsrud 2005).

In analyzing multimedia messages in interaction, it is important to keep in mind one restriction. When people are exchanging messages, they only know the messages sent so far. Even though the analyst has access through his data to the outcomes of what is going on, she should

Messages 3.4
The Giant Green Sociologist

Subject: On the Esplanade"I'm on the Esplanade! Cool!"

Message 3.5
(The Giant Green Sociologist, continued)

Subject: The Giant Green Sociologist
"STOMP!"
"What was that?"
"STOMP!"
"Run for your lives... it's... it's... the Giant Green Sociologist!"
"STOMP!"

not use her understanding as a resource in her work. Instead, the analysis has to work from the participants' perspective. When Tom sent Message 3.2, he did not know whether Ann Marie would respond, nor how she would design her response. However, people engaged in interaction in practical circumstances seldom take radical departures from what one could expect from certain response instructions, which almost always elicit certain responses. In conversation, greetings are responded to with greetings (Heritage 1989), questions with answers (Schegloff and Sacks 1973), and evaluations with assessments (Goodwin and Goodwin 1987). Any other response would lead to attempts to reinstate the "normal" line of action with various means, including repeating the greeting, asking whether the intended recipient did not hear the question, or whether he did not understand the evaluation. Thus, there is order in seemingly unordered activities, but this order is "locally" achieved: it is something accomplished just now, on just this particular occasion. In Garfinkel's (1967) terminology, people are held accountable for maintaining the perceived normalcy of action, and making it observable in what they do. Unless they do that, interaction becomes awkward, as people cannot trust their normal methods of action. More is at stake than mere momentary coordination.[2]

Mobile Multimedia as Endogenous Social Action

Ethnomethodology and its offshoot, conversation analysis, have sometimes been accused of forgetting society in their obstinate attempt to study action as it happens. However, as we have just seen, this is a grave misunderstanding. On the contrary, Garfinkel's early attempts to formulate a program for ethnomethodology was specifically designed to account for order in society, although not in terms familiar to most sociologists, who are typically more accustomed to think of order as something that is based on internalization of norms in society (Parsons 1937), or something that flows from social control (Black 1976). In contrast, ethnomethodology studies the practical grounds of ordinary actions—like multimedia messages—in order to account for the tremendous recurrent quality typical of ordinary society.

As noted in the previous section, in this vision, society is locally accomplished: order is in action, not in political structures, economy, or cultural norms. The only major requirement ethnomethodological studies have for analyzing society in action is that society cannot be separated from action, and then used to explain order, as this would mix causes and consequences. Instead, the analyst's task is to show how these structures are made relevant for action, and how they come to have consequences in action (Schegloff 1992).

From this perspective, an analysis of a political ideology would lead the analyst to study, say, the ways in which the notions of "gender," "Republican," "Democrat," and "insane" are occasioned in political discourse, and how these utterances (turns, texts, TV shows, etc.) are accepted, contested, and elaborated in subsequent actions (see Eglin and Hester 1999). In institutional and organizational contexts, these utterances—both their type and order—may be strictly allocated according to a certain pattern. For example, it is the prosecutor who asks questions, while the defendant's job is to answer them (Atkinson and Drew 1979). In ordinary action, there is more freedom of action; the next utterance is allocated on a local basis, in response to the previous utterance.

In analyzing mobile multimedia in ordinary action, this line of thinking means that we have to focus on how people occasion instances of social structure in their messages, and also what recipients do with them—ranging from being ignorant of to taking a strong stance on what has been taking place previously. Furthermore, this analysis has to be done without giving theoretical priority to any "level" of society. For example, categories of folk sociology extend from minuscule to global, "group" being used to describe small things, while "global economy" is used to denote things that affect the whole planet. People may, and do, use such terms in multimedia messages, and in so doing make issues in society and the world at large relevant and consequential for a brief moment.

However, these uses develop over time, as people learn new methods of action from each other. Perhaps the best example of the social basis of how methods of action develop is Orr's (1990; 1996) ethnography of copy machine repairmen. Orr worked with copy repair technicians, observing them at work, during breaks, and to some extent outside the workplace. He focused in particular on their incessant stories: even at lunch, technicians talked about individual machines. As he noted, these stories transmitted knowledge about the particulars of machines. Equipped with this knowledge, technicians were able to fix problems in machines even when company instructions and self-diagnostics built into machines did not provide answers. The best fixes became "war stories," told again and again to celebrate the technicians' identity (Orr 1996: 125–146). In other words, stories formulated and transmitted ethnomethods in the technicians' community.

To see how people's methodic base evolves in mobile multimedia, we may follow an instance analyzed previously by Koskinen et al. (2002).

The pilot group of their study realized that they could not only send images to other members of the group (and to outsiders), but they could also download images to their computers and manipulate them with trick effects. This invention led to a joking culture in which members constantly tried to beat others. However, as Chapter 12 shows in more detail, its origins were modest. One member experimented with an automatic signature on the mobile phone. He realized that he could add a photograph automatically to his messages instead of using a more typical textual signature consisting of his name, address and phone number. The next day, his idea took fire, when two other members developed visual signatures for themselves. However, they twisted the original idea: instead of self-portraits, they used the faces of Gillian Anderson and Liam Neeson (see Message 12.1). When seeing this message, other members of the group realized that they could use the fantasy worlds of popular culture as a lens through which to observe and report things in everyday life.

For example, the image in Message 3.4 shows a street scene in summer. As such, there is nothing special in this postcard-like message. However, as shown in Message 3.5, another member of the group rapidly replied with a manipulated image, to which he had attached a photograph of one of the researchers. The sender of the first message could hardly have predicted a response as creative as the Green Sociologist. Although the response maintained the original image, it set it in a new frame of reference in which the original image acquired a new meaning. For example, the city is no longer a beautiful object, but filled with horror. The streets, typically solid and reliable, are all of a sudden trembling, people are running for their lives, as the blue sky above the horizon is filled by the threatening giant. Although the original message provides a "gestalt contexture" (Gurwitsch 1964) by assembling the message elements intentionally to certain effect, recipients may reorganize these gestalt contextures instead of just going along with them.

As with Orr's technicians who tell stories, people who see examples like these in their phones simultaneously learn new methods of action. The history of use shapes future use. At one point in time, people use technology in certain ways. At a later point in time, however, they might use it differently, even when the people are the same and the situation is more or less similar: they simply have different methods at their disposal. Thus, although multimedia messaging is often based on the ordinary, age-old methods of action (Taylor and Harper 2002) familiar to us from innumerable occasions in everyday life, strikingly new developments may take place as well. Their value lies in that they make it possible to study how people create new ways of using their phones. Also, they show that even mundane, ordinary activities are achievements. If people do not discover new methods of action, there must be reasons for such conservatism.

Conclusions

Ethnomethodology and its offspring, conversation analysis, lead to a detailed study of action as it evolves turn by turn, with a focus on how people situate themselves in this evolving line of action. Such study aims at respecification of action as a locally organized natural activity (Garfinkel 1986; Sharrock and Button 1993: 167–168). This Chapter has respecified mobile multimedia as something that is inseparable from those human activities in which it participates. In Garfinkel's (1996) recent terminology, they make a pair: technology and human activities are irrevocably tied together, and need to be studied as such, not in isolation.

This Chapter has begun the task of recovering the work of multimedia messaging. We have seen that mobile multimedia has a complex methodic basis. First, to get at the specificities of mobile multimedia, we need to analyze the means of expression typical to that media, including the ways in which people exploit such traditional media forms as postcards and stories to their advantage, and communicate using bodily expressions instead of, say, just text. Second, we need to analyze mobile multimedia on a message-by-message basis as interaction. Third, these methods develop over time; people discover methods of action from each other. Mobile multimedia messaging, as understood in this book, is organized activity consisting of messages as well as replies and responses to them.

The perspective initially described in this Chapter provides an alternative to studies based on more traditional structural and psychological concepts. Thus, it does not necessarily contest early findings and arguments concerning mobile telephony. For example, it may well be that mutual entertainment proves to be the main "driver" of mobile multimedia in the future, as some design studies (Mäkelä et al. 2000; Frohlich 2004) and early studies (Koskinen et al. 2002; Scifo 2005; Ling and Julsrud 2005) have suggested. Also, there is little reason to doubt that boring situations of everyday life will be the "home base" of mobile multimedia, much like researchers on mobile phones claim (for example, Kopomaa 2000). It may also well be that mobile multimedia will be a major platform for the mobile Internet, bringing in benefits predicted in industry forecasts. If that is the case, it becomes more than a personal technology.

However, before accepting this conclusion, we need to situate mobile multimedia in society by studying it as practical activity instead of jumping to theoretical conclusions prematurely. When mobile multimedia is respecified as a naturally occurring activity, we get a more accurate description of it than with alternative theories.

Notes

1   Garfinkel develops the classic statement of 1967 in new directions in his more recent writings (Garfinkel 1996 and 2002).

2   As Rich Ling suggested to me, this seems to be common territory between the "genre" approach and the more ethnomethodological tack of analysis. In action, there is the necessity for maintaining the ability to account for actions. When grounded genres are seen as broad scripts that at once constrain the type of interaction, but also suggest further directions for it, they can be seen simply as ethnomethods.

Part II

Design Elements of Mobile Multimedia

4

Snapshots, Media, and Age-Old Practices

It has been argued that mobile multimedia provides people with a means to explore their surroundings visually and to exploit its features for the purposes of communication. For communication, people have at their disposal a set of methods that have their origins in various aspects of society. For example, they may use traditional media forms as templates for mobile visual communication. The modern world is rich in such traditional forms of media, ranging from postcards and B-movies to animations, news photographs, and images in fashion advertising. For anyone who has a mobile multimedia phone, such forms provide a stock of means for capturing things and events and for organizing messages into an intelligible form.

What explains the variation in how people design multimedia messages? Following insights from the sociology of technology (Bijker 1995), one possibility is the technology itself. The device suggests to people several possible precedents. Most obviously, the device can be seen either as a camera, a mobile phone with a text messaging feature, or a recorder (and increasingly, a video camera) (see Kasesniemi 2003). However, there are other possible sources of designs as well. For example, people may borrow techniques from mass media, the arts, as several students of virtual technologies have suggested (Ling and Julsrud 2005; Darley 2000). Also, they may simply take cues from ordinary life, as Berg et al. (2003) have suggested, including methods such as posing questions and getting answers to them. This Chapter surveys where people take their cues when designing multimedia messages.

Snapshot Photography Enters Multimedia

As Richard Chalfen (1987) notes, a good deal of ordinary photography can be characterized as part of the *Kodak Culture*. In contrast to more formal modes of photography inherited from the nineteenth century, the new Kodak cameras made it possible for people to capture photographs easily by just pushing a button. When practically no experience and knowledge of photography was needed to shoot photos, practically all ordinary areas of life opened to photography. The contrast to studio photography with its poses and portrait-like compositions could hardly be stronger (see also Bourdieu 1990).

Most things and events captured with multimedia phones fit this description easily. For example, Message 4.1 shows a young mother feeding a baby. The text places this snapshot at sea, indirectly revealing that the interior is a boat. Message 4.2, on the other hand, is a photograph of a colorfully dressed young man, who is laughing and carrying several stuffed animals in his arms. The text, logically enough, places the scene in an amusement park. Finally, the photograph of a cat in Message 4.3 is self-explanatory, not requiring an explanation.

Perhaps the most popular ordinary method for sharing traditional photographs has been the photo album (Gardner 1991; Frohlich et al.

Message 4.1
Anders to Lana

Mary and Sanna at sea

Message 4.2
Sam to Ari, Lara, and Tim

Beware of the Candy Man! Greetings from Linnanmäki! [Tivoli]

Message 4.3
Petri to Annemarie

((no text))

2002). The first Internet-based services for pictures taken with digital cameras were based on this metaphor. In *Mobile Image*, people were informed about the possibility of using Web albums such as *Zing.com* (now bankrupt) or *Kodak.com* for storing and sharing their images. With the exception of three members of the pilot group, no one in our data built WWW albums with their images. Still, something analogous was taking place in other groups, but on different, more situated premises. The most typical response to a mobile image was another mobile image of a similar topic. For example, when someone sent a picture of a cat, others typically responded with pictures of cats—or furry animals, if they were not cat people. This practice has been called "theme formation" (Koskinen and Kurvinen 2002). Theme-formation is familiar to us from traditional photo albums and WWW albums that are filled with photographs of childhood homes, friends, parents, spouses, pets, and travel and vacation photographs.

The best example of how theme-formation developed comes from the female group. "Boyfriends" became a prominent theme for photographing immediately. In fact, the very first image in this group was Kirsi's photograph of her boyfriend. With this message, she made boyfriends possible objects of photographing. In the four days after beginning, Mervi, Liisa, and Minna had responded with photographs of their boyfriends. Within a few days, "boyfriends" had become a shared focus of attention and an important common theme for the group. Importantly, participants recognized these themes. In interviews, we wanted to know whether these themes were set by agreement, or whether people just realized one day that their messages had become thematic (see Koskinen et al. 2002: 67–71):

Esko: Did you have common themes, that is, topics or themes, in your group?

Eija: Ehm. ... we did not agree on any theme in advance. But of course, there are certain themes like "Me and my boyfriend," and then there is "Me somewhere outside my home." I think there were terribly many messages that essentially said "Me somewhere."

Such "themes" become a platform for several "second-order" activities. Once a theme is recognizable, it is possible to take a stand towards it. One can join the theme, and thus show that one thinks it is important.

One can also develop the theme artistically or in some other systematic fashion. Recognizable themes also make satire and joking possible. In fact, there are rudiments of such everyday inventions throughout our data (see Koskinen et al. 2002: 69–71).

Systematic comparisons between these "mobile albums" and traditional photo albums do not exist, but it is possible to present a conjecture. Photographs in traditional albums are the result of prior photographic planning, and thus reflect traditional categories more than mobile albums, which are creations of the moment. As Eija's answer suggests, it is appropriate to talk about "themes" instead of "categories," and thus mark a difference between a looser sort of categorization-in-the-making in the wireless domain, and the more fixed category systems in traditional photo albums. Statistical studies of home albums largely concentrate on these themes (see Gardner 1991). Typically, they have been seen as reflections of cultural categories, and interpreted in terms of social structure—typically, in terms of gender, age, education, wealth, or discourse. However, in the context of mobile multimedia, it is better to see them as situated achievements rather than as something that is directed by traditional socio-economic or class variables.

Media Genres on the Phone: Picture-Based and Story-Based Genres

In some respects, mobile multimedia messaging goes beyond the Kodak culture. For one, people use some media genres in designing their messages (Ling and Julsrud 2005; see Darley 2000). Again, the role of text is crucial in turning snapshot-like photographs into these media genres, as I will call them following Ling and Julsrud's (2005) suggestive formulation. These genres can be classified into two main types. First, there are *picture-based genres*, consisting of postcard-like messages as the dominant form. As such, this category might contain other types of photographs, too, including news photographs, fashion photographs, pornography, furniture advertisements, and artistically influenced photographs, all easily available in everyday life. The second category consists of *story-based genres* in which photographs are situated in a story of some sort, including poetry, gossip columns, and various types of movie formats.

Picture-Based Genres

By far, the most typical genre used in constructing multimedia messages is the postcard (see Lehtonen et al. 2003; Ling and Julsrud 2005).

A typical postcard has a greeting, and a description of the sender's location and surroundings. Postcards typically are closed with a section of greetings, which typically consists of two parts, a greeting and a signature (Tainio 1999). In Message 4.4, Jari ("J") has sent a picture from a holiday trip in Italy. The attached text locates the picture in a certain country and elevation from sea level. In addition, it includes a relaxed explanation of the event: on a normal April working day in Helsinki, you do not get to "stuff your face" with "pizza, birra and grappa." On the other hand, the picture complements the text in many ways. In addition to proving that the sender is actually in Italy and that the weather is fine, it also shows what a relaxing life he is enjoying on his vacation. The message lacks unnecessary explanation and conveys a friendly atmosphere. It also has an informal signature: it has been sent to friends.

Mobile multimedia changes postcards in at least two ways. First, with a "hip top" multimedia device, one can produce the card instead of buying a commercial one. In a mobile postcard, not only the content, but also the picture is personal. The second difference to traditional postcards is more interesting, and is based on the technical possibility of sending the card. Many mobile postcards are spurs of the moment that would be impossible to share with the traditional mail-based process. For example,

Message 4.4
Postcard from Italy

Terde, at 1100 meters, +25C. Stuffed my face with pizza, birra and grappa. J

it would be difficult to imagine sending a postcard from Linnanmäki to friends who live in Helsinki, in which the amusement park is located. The place is familiar to anyone who has spent his or her childhood in Helsinki—or Finland, for that matter. It is the fact that one is there *right now* that justifies sending the message.

Out of other possible picture formats available for multimedia photographers, only few were encountered in the *Mobile Image* and *Radiolinja* data sets. With the exception of the pilot group in *Mobile Image*, there were no examples of news photographs or fashion photographs in these data sets. As Chapter 7 will show, several pictures were dubbed "art pictures" in these data sets. However, this label was given to pictures that were somehow beautiful, but incomprehensible; it was a method of "saving" certain images rather than a conscious effort to produce artistically interesting photos. In fact, the only magazine genre that was encountered in these data was pornography. Several participants, mostly men, took pictures from porn magazines, movies, and their own body parts. However, with the exception of a couple who once exchanged raunchy pictures while flirting, in all other cases in which the picture was pornographic, the text was not: the text turned these pictures into either teases or jokes. Pornographic pictures were used to produce a shock effect rather than for sexual stimulation. In terms of content, these pictures were largely similar to background images marketed by the porn industry. These messages show the importance of attending to all media elements in multimedia messages: although the visual genre was borrowed from media, textual content may do something else.

Story-Based Genres

Another media source from which people borrowed methods for designing multimedia messages is based on stories of various types. That is, the image (or images) are situated in a story line that gives them meaning. Images illustrate the story line, and sometimes make up its basis, but they are not understandable without the storyline. Typically, these were individual inventions, not more widely shared methods. Thus, while one participant sent poetic messages, another sent messages that borrowed from gossip columns, while a third borrowed from movies. The story line is the main feature that distinguishes story-based formats from postcards, which were used by practically all participants in both studies.

These story lines were based on several story genres, some based on literature, some on print media, and some on electric media. To take the example of literary genres, one young man sent several long poetic messages in an apparently flirtatious tone to two young women. Typically, he installed his profile in these messages in ways that visually elaborated the poem's content. For example, in one case, he wrote about his yearning to leave behind his boring life, and inserted a picture in which he was watching red clouds over the sea at sunset. However, after this poetic opening, he quickly proceeded to make arrangements for the next day. This particular poem was not the point of the message; rather, it served as an atmospheric opening only.

In contrast, gossip columns represent an example of how print media genres can be handy in designing messages. The best example comes from *Radiolinja*, in which one woman was sailing, and sent several pictures she dubbed "gossip" and "spying," perhaps reflecting unfamiliarity and moral hesitation with the device. In one message in particular, she sent pictures of two well-known actors whom she saw in a marina (Message 12.2 analyzes this example in more detail).

Other than these fairly simple story genres, some media genres are used to create considerably more complex messages, which may require planning, acting, staging, and a string of several messages to convey the message. The following story (Message 4.5) was shot several weeks earlier, but not sent until Midsummer night (see Koskinen et al. 2002: 55–61). Some people had already enquired about it, as can be deduced from the first line. The heading, "Murder at Lammassaari," makes the reader expect a murder mystery. The prologue tells the reader that a scratch on Eija's hand initiated the story. A blunder is also explained: the initial first shot was accidentally deleted. In the first image, we see a group of horrified people. They have witnessed bloodshed, which is proved in the next scene. In the last two shots, a body is found after which the murderer is seen running away. When the fourth and final image of the first message is reached the series of night images has been crafted into a movie-like story. The movie-like atmosphere is emphasized in the finale by talking about the Oscar gala, which places the story in the world of mainstream movies.

The Lammassaari Murder Story represents one of the few cases where the participants "wrote" a play that was immortalized with a camera. However, as this example shows, having access to mobile multimedia devices may provide people with the means to make art in and out of ordinary life. As such, this story suggests that some behaviors in the wireless domain fit what early literature on the cyberspace claimed (Murray 1999; Darley 2000).

Message 4.5
The Lammassaari Murder Story

Murder at Lammassaari: The long awaited horror movie shots!Unfortunately, I messed up and deleted the first image by accident (but I've heard I'm not the only clutz among us...). The first image was a picture of the murderer's hand the story got its start in a small scratch on Eija's hand sometime in the darkest hours of the night at the Lammassaari summer party.

1. Horror at Lammassaari: A murder has been committed!

2. A body in the grass (note the smile)

3. The body is found

4. The murderer runs for it

5. Plot climax: The murderer is caught...
(left, up, IK)

6. The murderer gets what he deserves - The Happy Ending (left, below)

7. The cinematographer wins an Oscar, responding to acclaim like a champion (below)

It is important, however, to keep in mind that this story is exceptional. In other data, there were few examples of consciously dramatized, acted, and reflective stories like this one. More typically, stories are shorter, and not scripted. They are more like typical youthful travel reports centered on one person's experiences. As in the *Lonely Planet*, these travelogues center on the sender's activities and often witty, slightly sarcàstic opinions about what has happened to them.

Age-Old, Ordinary Practices as Design Formats

Mobile multimedia builds still another set of practices. Namely, people borrow structures for designing messages from those methods of action they use in ordinary life in interacting with other people. Again, pictures as such use formats familiar to us from the *Kodak culture*, as Chalfen (1987) calls snapshot photography. Perhaps the best examples of such age-old practices (Taylor and Harper 2002) in multimedia data are greetings. Since greetings have already been analyzed in the previous Chapter, I will not return to them here. Instead, Message 4.6 provides an example of an invitation, while Message 4.7 is a mock call for help. In the picture is the cover of the most popular Finnish family game ever, using its Swedish name, *Afrikas Stjärna* (The Star of Africa). In previous chapters, we have already seen examples of gift-like messages and "exchanges." Other typical age-old practices in multimedia models are pieces of advice, where are you messages, instructions (for example, visual shopping lists), reminders, and "for your information" messages. Many of these practices are familiar from studies of text messages (Nurmela et al. 2000: 14).

Message 4.6
Markku to John

Hi! Are you in town? Are you coming for a beer?

Message 4.7
Anne to Leila

How do you play this??? Help!

A particularly prevalent set of age-old practices consists of reports of various sorts. As Okabe and Ito (2006) note, among peers people often report newsworthy things to others. This situation happens in the Finnish data as well. Some reports, again, may borrow from media formats. In one case, for example, Tina reports about swans she had seen in the same manner as in TV news when animals do something exceptional. However, more often people are simply either reporting what they are doing at the moment, where things are happening, or how they experience—or have experienced—some event or place. In Message 4.8, Ari sends an evaluation of his recent cruise, saying that he was disappointed in it. Finally, people also use age-old methods to make jokes. What could be more classical than a man dressed in women's clothing, as in the case of Ari wearing a bra next to a lake (Message 4.9)? Other age-old humor formats were mimicking animal sounds, mimicking children, putting words into children's and pets' mouths, all imaginable types of funny faces, and (usually phallic) sexual metaphors.

Messaging practices like these are based neither on photographic traditions nor on media. They go back to more basic forms of action known to people much before the advent of photography. Keeping eye contact while talking and making a joke by cross-dressing are not instances that were invented in photography. Yet, just as photographic and media practices, they guide the ways in which people use their devices both in capturing and designing messages.

Message 4.8
Ari to Sam and to Johan

Text: A disappointed cruise guest heading for new challenges. Audio (5 sec)01   Ari
Bla::::::h:::::,

Message 4.9
Ari to 10 people

It is always nice to swim.

Conclusions

Do people choose forms for multimedia messaging from the world of photography, from mobile telephony and text messaging, from media, or from just ordinary, "age-old" forms of action? This Chapter has shown that traces of all these traditions can be found in multimedia messages, and that they often take place in messages at the same time. In terms of how people use the camera, camera phones build on, and speed up the *Kodak culture*, in which photographs are objects of momentary fun and consumption rather than of more lasting value (cf. Chalfen 1987). However, people also borrow methods from mass media (Ling and Julsrud 2005) and from ordinary life (Taylor and Harper 2002).

Thus, multimedia messages exhibit several orderly properties at the same time. Ling and Julsrud's (2005) notion of "genres" is one of the first theoretical attempts to define this quality in theoretical terms. It has the benefits of being intuitive and having some explanatory power. However, such analysis also raises problems. First, it only accounts for a small portion of messages; not all messages can be described as genres. Also, as we have seen in Chapter 3, such analysis neglects many features of messages, including issues like greetings, signatures, questions embedded into messages, and the positioning of these items. Second, such analysis leads to problems in imagination. The researcher's task becomes one of identifying genres, describing them, and then showing that these genres are borrowed from culturally established ones. Since there are no lists of genres, the depth of such analysis depends ultimately on the researcher's imaginative capacity. The third problem is a consequence of the previous one: taking this framework seriously would reduce analysis of multimedia to an endless list of genres. The final problem is that this tack treats people as "cultural dopes" (Garfinkel 1967: 68–69), whose actions are determined by a genre, a ghost in the machine, instead of their own mindful behavior.

This is not to say that genre analysis is useless. On the contrary. However, analyzing traditional media forms as ethnomethods gives genres a specific role. They are resources for action. People know them, and can use them to structure their actions. Also, genres are easy to comprehend, and thus safe for senders, who do not have to be afraid of getting angry or frustrated responses. Furthermore, they are based on generations of commercial and professional work. They are able to convey complex meanings in a compact form. Finally, they provide people with methods for organizing social occasions. The Lammassaari Murder Story is a case in point. With this story, six people were able to organize having fun into a special, prolonged experience that required planning, rehearsing roles, and acting the story for the camera. The story was talked about among friends, who were eager to see it in their mailboxes.

5

Sound in Mobile Multimedia

Sound, like text, can be used to capture ideas, intentions, rational trains of thought, and other forms of everyday impressions. In sending greetings, news, questions and sometimes humor, sound often works better than text in SMS or "voiceless" MMS. There are two types of audible sound in messages. First, there are "foreground" sounds: these are the most prominent sound elements in the message. Typically, the foreground is composed of one or two spoken utterances. People may also add color and meaning to messages by, for instance, making ironic or humorous statements next to the message (see Battarbee and Koskinen 2004). Second, the microphone also captures "ambient" sounds: in the background of the message, there are sounds from the cityscape, people, animals, objects, music, street noise, sounds of traffic, people talking, and footsteps on the sidewalk. These sounds are typically—but not necessarily—attached to messages unintentionally.

How understanding evolves essentially depends on how sound develops (see Nyíri 2002 for a similar point regarding animations; for video, Francis and Hart 1997; Ihde 1976 gives a phenomenological statement). When listening, the listeners are situated in a lived organization that existed at the time of capture. Depending on how sound develops, action is available from ambient sound in many ways. For instance, people can get an understanding of what is going on by hearing how people participate in it. Hearing an order, price, handing over money and thank yous tell about a routine commercial transaction. Baby talk followed by laughter tells about interacting with a baby. Thus, although any element in a multimedia message is indexical and can be heard in many ways, this is not typical of ordinary action. Each element in the message—including ambient sounds—gets a definite meaning from other elements in the message in a "reflexive" fashion (see Garfinkel 1967: 1–11).

Sound in the Foreground

In each message in these data, there is a dominating sound element that is available to the recipient. Typically, this element is talk. What does talk do in mobile multimedia messaging? What is its main value in relation to phone calls?

By far, most important with foreground sound are greetings of various sorts. These range from birthday greetings to have a nice day messages. To give an example of a greeting, the following message is a birthday greeting to Markku, who is turning thirty. This example is essentially a singing postcard. In it, Anne and her boyfriend sing the clichéd Happy Birthday (in Finnish) to Markku, add a picture of flowers, and also add a textual greeting to the message. We also hear how two people react to their own performance: he is initially out of tune and rhythm, which she acknowledges with laughter tokens while singing. The pair accounts for their flawed performance with the signature "honeytones," which makes the message jocular: this is a simple tune, but so clearly out of rhythm and melody that the senders account for these flaws with self-irony (Message 5.1).

The second prominent use of sound in the foreground is for sound samples (see Frohlich and Tallyn 1999). Typically, sampled were babies (see Message 5.4) and friends. A third type of usage is imitating human or animal voices. For example, in one message, there is a woman sleeping in a car. The audio mimics loud snoring. In another case, the object of imitation is an ostrich; the sender had visited an ostrich farm. The fourth practice is more instrumental, where voice is used instead of a call to deliver practical information or to coordinate get-togethers. However, there are only a few cases in which audio files were used for such practical purposes. The final and most prominent, way to use sound in the message foreground is to use it as an "emotion enhancer": sound describes the sender's feelings. Interestingly, this usage has a syntax-like format. Most typically, there is a picture of the sender's face, with some kind of yell or other emotionally loaded sound added. For example, Arne once sent a message evaluating his recent cruise by noting in text that he was disappointed and ready for further adventure. The sound was a loud "Bla::::::,h::::," which leaves little doubt about how his cruise had gone. Interestingly, explanatory uses of voice—annotating images with words—are nonexistent in these data (see Frohlich and Tallyn 1999; Frohlich et al. 2002).

Message 5.1
Happy birthday

Text: May you have a sunny 30th birthday! Br. Honeytones

01	Woman ((singing)) Happy bir[thday to you, happy
02	Man [*day to you ((joins
03	Woman =[Birt(h)(h)hday to you, happy birthday to Markku,h
04	Man [((Singing, first out of tune and rhythm — — — — —))
05	Woman =[Happy /birthday] to you ((at the end, voice is too high))
06	Man [((— — — — — — — — —))]

Ambient sound: no recognizable ambient sound.

Note also how talk may make the sender's mood, emotions and attitude available to recipients. For example, in Message 5.1, it is not just the picture, the very act of sending a greeting card, and singing that make the message joyful. We can also hear how the singers act in unison, amusing each other as they go along. In particular, she almost bursts into laughter when he joins her shyly and out-of-tune. Part of the fun of an audio message is that whoever happens to hear it can also hear how the people who design the message relate emotionally and socially to their own actions.

Background Sound: Hearing Place in Ambient Sound

The soundscape in mobile multimedia is considerably more complex than the foreground. By listening to the foreground only, recipients not only hear the message, but also get an idea of what the sender has intended to say, his mood, how he has assessed his experiences, his wit, and also his company. However, when recipients turn their attention to a background pattern rather than the evidence in the foreground, they get access to a host of other, more contextual aspects of what is going on.

In the following, there are two minimal cases, one with non-human, another with a human ambient sound. In Message 5.2, there is an obscure item in the photograph. The text tells that there is fly fishing gear in the image. Laughter in the foreground is so loud and exaggerated that the sender's joy cannot go unnoticed. The sound may describe the long wait before the purchase, or about future days spent fishing. Most likely, it tells both things simultaneously.

The ambient sound is a strong echo typical of a room that is nearly empty. The message is situated inside rather than outside. There are no sounds of the wind or the street; instead, the message is compiled in a quiet environment. The sender is also apparently alone in the room. The interior can be heard from several features of the soundscape: nobody

Message 5.2
Fly Fishing Gear

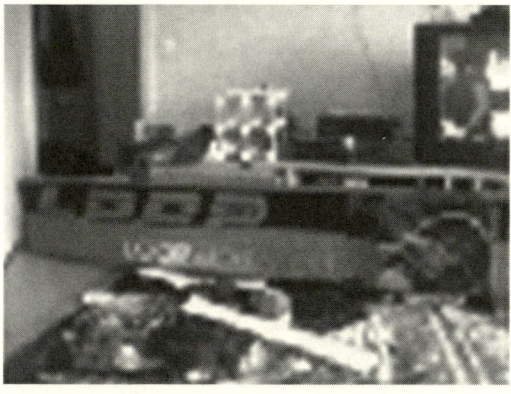

Text: I bought fly fishing equipment.

01   Man   HEH HEH HEH HEH HEH
02   <HE HE HE HE HE HEE::e:: hoe:::.>

Ambient sound all along: strong echo, apparently alone in a room.

joins him, the sounds of the city are outside the audible horizon, and there is no apparent direction to the sound. Given the picture that shows consumer electronics in a messy room, a good guess is that the picture is taken in John's home (comp. to Ihde 1976: 60–71, 106–108).

In the next example (Message 5.3), the action is easy enough to understand from the point of the message. Jaana, given certain specifications by Anne, has promised to check the cover for a cushion in a shop, and has promised to buy it. In the shop, Jaana learns that the color Anne wants is unavailable. She captures an image and sends it, with an audio clip querying whether she should buy it anyway. Interestingly, Jaana also corrects an element in the image with audio (see Frohlich and Tallyn 1999) when she notes that the colors are reproduced badly in the photograph. She asks for

Message 5.3
Cushion Covers

Text:((No text))

01 Woman	.pth Here I am, Anne (.) D'you see the middle one of
02	these cushion covers (.) the colors are shown pretty
03	badly?,
04	(.)
05	But ehm h (.) this blue is quite pretty?, /But
06	ehm .h [send me a message
07 Ambient	[((commercial announcement in the background))
08 Woman	I'll take it with me:::,h (.) so do you wa:nt
09	it or not (.)
10	/Bye h

Quiet ambient sound all along: crowd noise, echo.

a quick reply before closing the message with a goodbye; we do not have access to the reply that, if it came, was probably a call. This message is a part of a more extended action that has a history and a future course.

Here the ambient sound consists of background noise and a commercial announcement. Notice that there is no mention of *where* Jaana is shopping. It could be any commercial venue—a shopping mall, department store, or just a shop. As the "here I am" in the opening of the message implies, Jaana and Anne have discussed Jaana's going to the mall previously, so that there is no need to identify the place. Still, ambient sound manages to situate the message in a shopping mall, for two reasons. First, the background noise tells from the very beginning that the place is large. There is a strong echo in the sound, and the talking crowd is sizeable, thus ruling out a local shop or a boutique. When the commercial announcement comes in after 12 seconds, the remaining alternatives are either a shopping mall or a large department store. In Message 5.2, no similar stepwise development took place in the ambient sound.

These cases show how audio and other multimedia elements work together to situate action in a certain place. Importantly, place tells about action: people may infer what others are doing *from* knowledge of the place. In the second example, the sender is in a shopping mall; apparently, shopping is the default activity and mindset there. When the sender is in a calm, peaceful setting, what takes place there is more ambiguous. However, people may also infer place from activity. In the shopping mall case, there are no identifiers of place, but we still manage to hear it that way. Importantly, certain places are linked to certain activities. When people hear that someone is in a shopping mall or a bar, they can figure out with good confidence what he or she is doing there, and also his or her mindset (see Drew 1978 for how places and geography function in talk; a more formal treatment is Schegloff 1972: 96–106). In this sense, even a minimalist ambient soundscape does important work in mobile multimedia messaging.

It is also worth noticing how Jaana carefully manages her relationship with Anne by avoiding making taste an issue. She does not directly ask whether Anne would like to have the cushion, but asks her opinion. She also uses rising question intonation and softens her judgment about the color into "pretty blue" instead of making a categorical judgment about the color. Finally, she asks her response before buying the cover. Through careful wording, utterance construction, and intonation, she avoids pushing her agenda, and leaves all decisions to Anne. Without such precautions, she might appear pushy and impatient.

Hearing Interaction

Ambient sound may also make social action available for the hearer. In some cases, hearing the ambient sound tells us vividly what is going on regardless of text or the fact that in *Radiolinja*, all messages contained only still images. In Message 5.1, we saw how two people took each other's orientations into account while singing a birthday song. In the following message (Message 5.4), there is a picture of a baby against blue water, suggesting that the image was taken in a swimming hall. This is

Message 5.4
Baby Talk

Text:Greetings from East Centre, br. Zoey

01 Baby	((Quiet noise, attempts to talk))
02	(2.0)
03 Woman	((Laughs))
04 Woman	((Talks to other adults in the background, words
05	inaudible))
06	(1.0)
07 Woman	Oh look, here it (comes) ((talks to adults))
08	(1.0)
09 Baby	((Talks louder))
10 Woman	((Talks, followed by laughter, inaudible))
11	(1.0)
12 Baby	((Cries loud, almost starts to scream))
13 Woman	And then we take the bott— ((sound cut off))

Ambient sound all along: Quiet talk by many people, a café—like sound that disappears when the baby starts to talk and cry, or the mother talks loud.

confirmed by the text, which situates the message in the "East Centre," a large shopping mall area roughly 10 km east of downtown Helsinki. Near the mall, there is a public swimming pool, which also organizes baby swimming. On the top, the whole message is offered as a "Greeting," sent to ten persons.

The camera has captured a laughing baby, but the sound tells more about what is going on in the scene, if we analyze the directionality of the sound (comp. Ihde 1976: 74–76). At first, we hear the sounds of the baby and a few adults. The baby "Zoey" (nickname) is swimming with her mother, and makes cheerful noises all along. The adults nearby are laughing, apparently amused by the baby. At the end of the message Zoey gets food from a bottle. For the sender, the message becomes a vehicle for sharing a delightful experience, which also justifies sending the message.

But this is the foreground sound only. An analysis of how the ambient sound develops and is directed gives us a detailed idea of what is going on. We first hear a baby attempting to talk, and see a young man in the background (who he is remains unclear). Next a woman laughs near the microphone. It is at this moment that we first hear a key element of the social organization: it is the baby's mom. Located next to the microphone, these two become hearably units of a pair (see Sacks 1972a, 1972b). After approximately 7 seconds, the mother again talks near the microphone. After 11 seconds, she turns her head away from the microphone and talks to the other adults, who respond to her. By now, all participants are known. However, the episode gets to a second phase when Zoey starts her baby talk again (after about 13 seconds). In response, the mother talks to other adults, and laughs briefly with them. After 2 seconds, Zoey again starts to cry, this time loudly. The mother takes this as a sign of hunger, and starts to feed her (24 seconds). Even though this is not mentioned anywhere in the message, we hear how the mother Susan keeps Zoey in her arms and feeds her.

Message 5.4 provides an example of how people can use common-sense knowledge of social structures (Garfinkel 1967: 76–103) to make sense of what they hear. This scene tells not only about how the mother and baby interact, but also about their company and its mood: they are with other adults, who share the mother's joy rather than remain merely bystanders. We can also follow the mother's orientation from sound even though we have no idea of her interlocutors or how they are placed around her. Recipients of the message not only hear several voices, but they also hear a key feature of ongoing social organization. At first, the mother tries to get the baby to talk to the microphone. When she is successful, she is able to direct her attention to her adult company for a moment before the baby catches her attention again by getting hungry. Here, the ambient sound introduces a social dimension to the message, tells about its character, and tells about how the mother and the baby allocate their involvement between each other and the social surroundings.

How Recipients Make Sense of Sound

By now we have seen that a multimedia message with an audio file creates a rich, multisensorial environment for the recipient. Sound files take the recipients beyond the visual: they give them access to several things that are unavailable in pictures and text. In this section, we will focus on how recipients orient to sound and what they do with it. The focus is on what features of sound the recipients attend to, and what features they pick up as key elements in their response.

Message 5.5
Painting

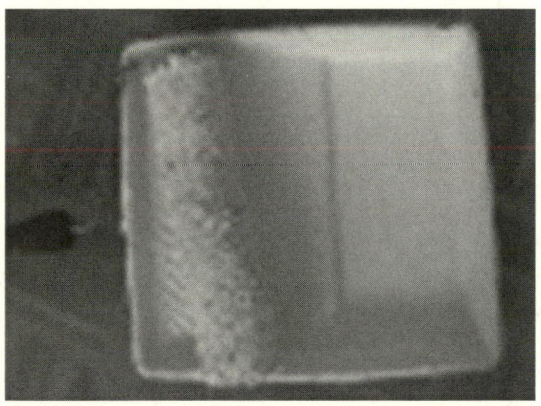

Text:((No text))

01 Man	Greetings?, (again from) the:?, (w)ork camp
02	in Mellunmäki?, (.) Have fun shopping
03	at the East Centre Mall.
04	(.)
05	/By:e:?,

Ambient sound all along: strong echo, apparently a quiet and empty room.

The recipients treat the foreground differently from ambient sound. Whenever an audio message is responded to, the response is targeted at the message rather than the ambient element. Recipient analysis focuses on the message, ratifying it as the key element in the message. For example, Arne responds to Susan's Message 5.4 with Message 5.5. The response is a simple return greeting, with a picture of a paint roller and a spoken joke about his present surroundings as a "work camp." Thus, he responds to a textual element rather than the sound. This is a more general feature of audio responses. People respond to the *act* in the previous message rather than to the sound. However, the choice of the response method is conditioned by the previous message. Audio elements are used in responses to audio messages.

There was only one case in which an ambient sound was targeted in response. Kai sent Thomas greetings from the bar of a cruise ship with a picture of a glass of wine. He also did two other things: he presented the picture as a riddle, and sent an audio sample from "the artist of the night, Kai Mäki." In the audio someone was singing "Who'll Stop the Rain" by Creedence Clearwater Revival. In text, Thomas's response to the riddle was "red wine," but he added that he "could not make sense of the sound," which is thus pointed out as a key unintelligible element in Kai's message. In effect, Thomas holds Kai accountable for making sure that the sound makes sense with a possible repair initiation. When sounds are specifically pointed out as important elements in messages, the senders ought to make sure that they are clear and understandable. These messages are reproduced in Chapter 7.

Although recipients mainly respond to the act done in talk, there are a few cases in which they analyze the speaker's mood and feeling from what they hear. Here we see the documentary method of interpretation at work (Garfinkel 1967). For example, in one instance, John sent a message telling that his summer holiday had just started. He also added a loud yell "/Jabujab<u>u</u>::, (.) /Ji:::ha::::," to the message to describe his feelings. Laura responded to John's announcement a few hours later with a spoken greeting card with an audio file and a graphic image. In the audio she sent her wishes to John with a ".hhh /H<u>a</u>ve a w<u>i</u>ld ri\deon your /h<u>oliday</u>: (.) John (0.3) /Ci:\ao." The graphic depicted a cocktail glass taken from the phone's photo library, showing her understanding of what will make John's holiday "a wild ride": having cocktails (and other drinks). Notice that the projected drinking spree is not available in John's message. Instead, she reads John's mood and his intention of spending time in bars indirectly from voice and text. It is John's joyous, loud yell that suggests this interpretation.

However, in general, there were few responses in these data. Sound is treated as a practical, non-problematic element. In contrast, almost all photographs are explicated in one way or another: both senders and recipients treat photographs as more ambiguous than sound (see Koskinen 2005). This is a major difference to Frohlich (2004), whose studies specifically focused on the uses of audio in augmenting photographs. One reason for this difference may be that in contrast to Frohlich's study, sounds in *Radiolinja* were ordinary and easy to understand. People face no difficulties in understanding echo or ambient talk in the background of a greeting. As these sounds came from familiar locations such as the senders' homes and shopping malls, they are not storyable like sounds from, say, a holiday trip to Poland, London, or a trek to the mountains (Frohlich 2004: 54–65). Another probable reason is that multimedia messages are typically viewed alone while in Frohlich's study, there were usually several people reviewing the audiophotographs (see Frohlich et al. 2002). In any case, it is important to notice that even though the users are not phenomenologists but orient to sound in practical terms, sound works well for them in multimedia messaging.

Conclusion

Unlike portable music devices such as the Walkman that people use to restructure their sonic experience while on the move (for instance, Hosokawa 1984; du Gay et al. 1997; Bull 2000; Thibaud 2003), mobile multimedia gives people new means to observe and report their activities and experiences with the environment (see Koskinen et al. 2002; Koskinen 2005; Okabe and Ito 2004; Ling and Julsrud 2005; Scifo 2005). This Chapter has focused on one aspect of the "hip top" multimedia environment only: the uses of audio capacity. The focus has been first on how people use sound in the foreground of the message and second on how they use ambient sound. In the foreground, audio files are used for various purposes, ranging from greetings to sending sound samples, imitations of animal and humans, and communicating emotions. They could also be used as an alternative to a phone call or a voice mail message. Typically, audio was used to initiate action rather than to respond to ongoing lines of action. We have seen that people use sound in a methodic fashion in their messages.

As Frohlich and Tallyn (1999) suggest, audio "augments" images in many ways: it adds life to images, allowing people to communicate more fully non-tangible qualities of action and context. However, we have also seen that it gives recipients a nuanced access to place and interaction, and allows a host of inferences about what is going on in the message. It would be hard to communicate all these meanings with text alone, as in SMS, or even with photographs augmented with text. Audio capability is a significant addition to the methodic repertoire of people using mobile multimedia.

Given that sound has an impressive expressive and interpretive potential, why are there so few audio messages? With further research pending, I can present a few conjectures. First, the voice mail culture has not been a standard part of life in Helsinki. Also, the phone function is the more obvious choice when one wants to talk. Second, sound is not a part of the considerably more lively text messaging culture (see Kasesniemi 2003; Lorente 2002). People in our data used MMS essentially to augment text messages with photographs. Sound is not a natural component of either textual or still images. The third cue lies in an analysis of responses: the sound world in mobile multimedia is largely self-evident and taken for granted. Here the difference to Frohlich (2004) is illustrative: for example, in his data, ambient sounds were typically from trips to unfamiliar places, or places dense with memories. The *Radiolinja* data is from places with a familiar soundscape that, consequently, was too unremarkable to be communicated. In sum, the audio function was something to be discovered: in the *Radiolinja* data, only one group discovered sound, which then became a standard part of its communication repertoire. It may be that people associate sound with moving pictures, but not still pictures. Also, using all the media available may be just a bother: before sending a message, one has to capture a photograph, record and save a sound file, design the message, write a text, and then search the sound file and add it to the message. Only then, is it available for preview and for sending. There are too many steps in this process as compared to a standard text message.

The data pose some obvious limitations on an attempt to generalize these results to future mass-market phenomena. First, the study is from the very first months when mobile multimedia came on the market. Secondly, the number of cases analyzed is small. However, these are not crucial issues in terms of the validity of the present analysis. Although these data are from the early days of mobile multimedia, users were ordinary, not professionals in information technology, sound production, or photography. The small number of cases limits the analysis, but does not make these observations wrong: I am here describing ordinary practices that no doubt will be found in larger data sets in the future. Larger data will in all likelihood reveal more nuances of audio use, but this does not threaten the validity of the present analysis.

Thus, the analysis shows just how rich a method audio is, even when used by ordinary people with no training in creating, analyzing, interpreting, or planning audio clips. The analysis, of course, is ultimately an attempt to explicate ways in which audio is used methodically in ordinary life. The final objective of this Chapter has been excavating minuscule practices that are often so simple that they are taken for granted and consequently go largely unnoticed in everyday life and in sociology alike.

6

Gestures, Faces, and Bodies as Communicative Resources

This Chapter takes a closer look at another novelty of multimedia messaging, namely how people use the body in designing messages. Faces and other body parts are ubiquitous in multimedia messages, and are used in several ways in communication. In industry scenarios, the possibility to augment mobile communication with pictures of the "speaker" widens the channel significantly, making interaction more natural than with mere voice and text. For example, video calls may be particularly useful for the hearing impaired (Kasesniemi et al. 2003). There are people who use such services, but by comparison to text messaging or even multimedia messaging service (MMS), their use was still very limited. For example, in early 2005, Swedish Television reported that there were slightly over 4,000 Swedish users of video calls in October 2004.

Although video has not caught up, something similar to video has been taking place in ordinary multimedia messaging service for several years. Gestures and body positions are critical issues in talk (for example, Goodwin 1981; Kendon 2004). Much like the cultural environment analyzed in the previous Chapter, gestures and the body are often made use of in mobile multimedia through still images.

A look back to previous chapters shows that people and bodies have some role in about half of all messages. Minimally, they appear as scenic elements in the background, or as objects of identification. This Chapter focuses on more expressive uses of the body, studies the relationship of the body to space and "props." It also studies the implicit uses of body in multimedia, and finally, focuses on how bodies are used in responses.

Gestures and Facial Expressions as Design Features

Previous chapters have already shown certain uses of the body in mobile multimedia. At the more minimal end, bodies appear in multimedia messages as a scenic feature in the background of a message. However, bodies and their parts have more expressive uses as well. People use their bodies in many ways to enhance or augment messages with conventional gestures. In the following case, a young man staged a story of his weekend activities. The story consisted of six messages, each showing pieces of a woman's clothing and underwear. It culminated in a photograph of her foot under a blanket, after which it was closed with Message 6.1, in which John uses a conventional symbol to evaluate his experience.

Other gestures done with hands were thumbs down, waves for greetings (Message 3.3), and the middle finger. The latter typically appeared in humorous contexts, for example, in holiday greeting cards. In a few messages, fingers were also painted so that they looked like smiling faces or conveyed messages in text (see Message 9.1). These gestures

Message 6.1
Thumbs Up

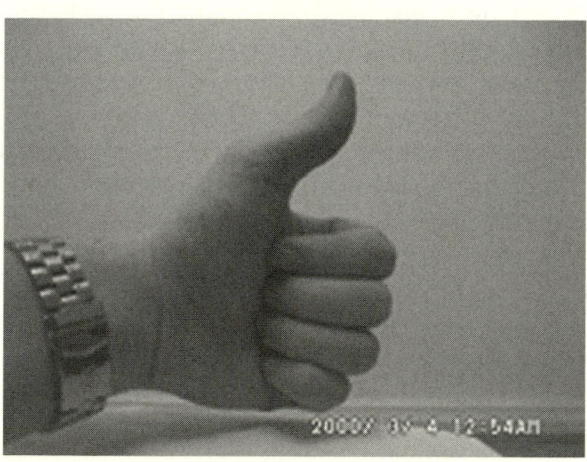

Overall, a very pleasant experience
John

are familiar from ordinary life; some would have been recognizable in Ancient Rome.

To illustrate how a more complex gesture works, let us consider the following two messages. In Message 6.2, four young women are in a cab going to a party. They call themselves "Barbies," with slight sexual overtone, and ask Markku to pay special attention to "Patsy's" (Mari's nickname) cleavage. In Message 6.3, Markku shows "embarrassment," and "demands" that someone cover up the cleavage, and enriches the response with a picture in which he covers his eyes, as if he has just seen something horrible.

Markku's gesture suggests several things. The gesture is familiar from several sources. When something is too awful and scary to watch without disgust and revolt, actors in horror movies hide their faces like Markku. This reaction is also typical to situations in which one is faced with nudity by accident. Either way, with his gesture, he suggests that "Patsy's" cleavage is so courageous that he can only look away.

Messages 6.2
Patsy's Cleavage

By Leila 02/7/18 19:13 pm.
Barbies in taxi. Note Patsy's cleavage

Message 6.3
Response to the Cleavage Message

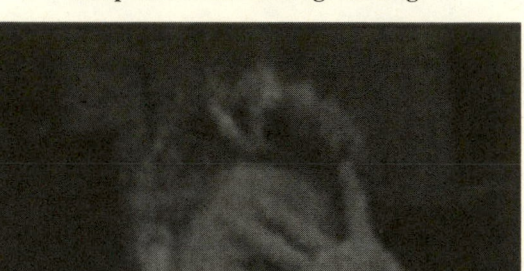

By Markku 02/7/18 19:43 pm:
The starry-eyed fairy girl gave me such a humongous compliment that I got pretty flushed and embarrassed... Hmmm... Have fun but, for God's sake, cover up Patsee's cleavage with a safety pin or something.

In addition to hands and fingers, faces provide a host of conventional methods for making moods and intentions available. In particular, faces are used to express emotions and moods. In one simple instance, John, a young man, declared the start of his vacation with a photograph of a smiling face shouting "/Jabujab<u>u::</u>, (.) /Ji:::ha:::::,," probably taken from the Flintstones. Message 6.4 is a more complicated case. Here Leena sends a greeting augmented with another conventional symbol of the good life, a glass of sparkling wine, and also a smiling face that confirms the feeling. Furthermore, two friends are visiting, and she tells about how she is waiting for the recipients to join in the holiday mood.

Faces and their parts were pictured to express feelings such as being sorry and missing the loved one, too. Still, faces do more than communicate emotions and moods. For instance, with a photograph of a furrowed forehead, one person mimicked the hard thinking suitable for a "professor" or a would-be Sherlock Holmes. Also, there is also a whole class of funny faces used to delight the recipient. For example, when one manages to take a photograph of a particularly funny facial expression, perhaps enhanced with a fake moustache or a pair of old-fashioned eyeglasses, the photograph can be sent to others to amuse them or to elicit a (mock) horrified response.

Message 6.4
Sparkling

Subject: Greetings from Kesäjärvi! No text.
Audio file:

01 Woman	So, greetings from here, our hot summer
02	garden, from Kesäjärvi. Having a glass of
03	sparkling. Leena and Pate are visiting,
04	lovely. See you tomorrow then, welcome!"

The Body in Space: Places, Interiors, Props

When discussing the uses of sound in the previous Chapter, I argued that sound goes beyond the image making horizons and environments available in a richer way than mere image. I also showed how this awareness of the environment changes the way in which the recipients understand the message. Something similar happens with gestures and other uses of bodies. In mobile multimedia messages, people are often situated in an environment that gives meaning to their action: the same gesture or body position means different things in different environments. Thus, the recipient can read what is going on in the image from this mixture of action and environment. For example, certain actions and moods "go with" certain places and environments. (See Schegloff 1972: 96–106; Drew 1978.)

Take the following case as an example. At 10:12, Pauli sent a message to Markku, with a photograph of a sunny marina with boats and blue sky in the background, and text saying "It's always fun at work, isn't it?" In response to this apparent tease, Markku confirms the query with "Really fun…" (Message 6.5). Markku's dry response comes to have sarcastic overtones partly because of the three dots that suggest that he is not in the mood to talk about what he is doing just then. Importantly, he adds a photograph from an office. In this photograph, two people are sitting at their desks, absorbed in their work. They have standard office furniture, and no windows bringing the summer into the office. The two workers have no face or personality. Few environments are less exciting than this one when compared to the sunny, enjoyable marina pictured by Pauli.

Also people may come to act as props. They are often made into symbols for communication. Pauli continued his work theme in another message to Markku a week later. This time he sent a photograph of an older man with a grey moustache and expensive-looking eyeglasses. He was sitting in the back seat of a car, and had a calm expression on his face. This grandfather figure turns out to be something else in this message, when Pauli puts the command "get back from vacation, now" in his mouth. He comes to stand for authority, even though he is dressed informally, with his collar open.

**Message 6.5
Fun in the Office**

Really fun..

However, most props are inanimate. Perhaps the most potent prop in the *Radiolinja* data is beer and wine. The data is from the particularly hot summer of 2002, and alcohol was present in many messages, either in text, or as an environmental element. A bottle of beer or wine efficiently situates action to leisurely activities, typically having good time with friends (comp. Koskinen et al. 2002: 48; Message 4.4).

The Body as an Implicit Background Feature

In his seminal *The Phenomenology of Perception*, the philosopher Maurice Merleau-Ponty tied perception to the body with the simple example of his apartment. His argument was that in ordinary life, people do not have access to a bird's-eye view of the apartment. Instead, their view is constituted in their activities from a variety of angles and viewpoints, depending on their current concerns and intentions (Merleau-Ponty 1986: 203). The point is that perception is tied to bodily activities: there is no transcendental point of view, knowing subject, or *cogito* in traditional philosophical language. When I walk around a statue or a building, I face surprises all along the way: new angles, new plays of light, new harmonies appear. If I stop at any point, I realize that perception is tied to our body. This point applies to all perception, not just to apartments and statues, but also to our experience of a piece of jewelry, or the town of Manila in the Philippines. The body interacts with things around us, and part of this interaction may enter messages as well.

As an example of how bodies are tied to perception, we can follow how the most talkative person in the *Radiolinja* data, Markku, reported his trip to the provincial town of Vaasa on the Finnish West Coast. He left for Vaasa at noon on July 12, and returned late in the evening on July 15. During his trip, he sent eleven messages with images. However, some of these messages were sent to several people; in all, he reported on his trip with 25 messages. In this string of messages, he described several activities and observations to his friends in three scenes. The first scene was the trip from Helsinki to Vaasa. The first message to Leila was from the main railway station in Helsinki, and the second one to John was sent from train. The Vaasa scene consisted of six messages describing a rabbit, several friends, cars, and an incident in which an "older lady" had ruffled his hair, almost causing a fight with her husband. The return-to-Helsinki scene consisted of four messages sent to various recipients, all taken from the train.

This message series situates Markku in several places, ranging from the main railway station in Helsinki to an unspecified "house" with rabbits, to a bar in Vaasa, and to an evening train back to Helsinki. In each message, it was the text that tied the images to certain places and activities. However, many of these places and activities are familiar to anyone. When we see a photograph of someone driving an old Volkswagen, we know that Markku is sitting in the back seat. We also know what happens in bars and trains, and can easily picture his activities in these contexts. The train scenes are from fairly standardized environments in which Markku does not move. The Vaasa scene, in contrast, is livelier. Markku's perception of the town is irrevocably tied to his movement and company in that town. Still, even in the train scenes, his perception is tied to his situation. Should he have been walking around in the train, or visited its restaurant, his perception would have been different from one concentrating on scenery shot from his seat.

The recipient has access to some of this bodily work through multimedia messages. He or she has to reconstruct Markku's bodily movements from bits and pieces in the message. Such recipient inferences are available in messages, whether in questions, comments, queries, or teases. In the Vaasa episode, Markku sent a photograph of Näsinneula, an observation tower located in Tampere, Finland's second largest city. It took only 8 minutes before he got a return message from John from a bar in Tampere asking whether he was in town. The message suggested to John that Markku is around and available for a chat over a glass of beer. However, his inference was not warranted: there was a delay of a few minutes between taking the photograph and sending it to John. Markku had already passed the town when he sent the message.

Often, the sender's body remains a presupposed but not seen feature of the setting (comp. Koskinen and Kurvinen 2002: 122–123). This is the case in three earlier messages in this Chapter: Patsy's Cleavage (Message 6.2), Sparkling (Message 6.4), and Fun in the Office (Message 6.5). However, even though the photographer is not seen in these messages, they document her action in several ways. The difference between Messages 6.4 and 6.5 is telling. In the former, the photographer was fairly near the lady in the photograph. In the latter, the distance from the photographer to the target is more remote and far less intimate. It is through distance and camera angles that pictures tell about what kinds of views the photographer is witnessing.

Another item worth noting is that the camera phone often acts like a mirror. With it, people may stage and capture their own actions and use them in communication. Message 6.3 is a particularly good example of such use. In that message, Markku jokingly showed his panic reaction to "Patsy's" cleavage. Notice how he holds his camera in his right hand at arm's length, while he uses his face and left hand to create an impression of a scare reaction. With a camera phone, one can stage, rehearse, and document one's reactions until they are satisfactory, and share only successful shots.

Textual and Bodily Responses to Bodily Action

In most cases, people respond to messages that picture gestures and bodies by focusing on action rather than gestures and bodies as such. Typically, the response is textual and targets what was said in the text. The main exception is compliments on beautiful pictures, typically sent by men to women. In these cases, the recipient sends a picture of his torso or smiling face rather than designs a specifically planned bodily response to the preceding message. Still, responses to bodily messages may also be based on bodily formats. For example, Markku's scare reaction to Patsy's cleavage in Message 6.3 is one of the few cases in which a gesture builds directly on a body-related element in the previous message. Even in this case, however, the reason for paying attention to the cleavage was textual rather than the photograph as such.

However, at least two specifically bodily response formats exist. First, in some responses, gestures and facial expressions substitute for text in conveying meaning. The following instance is a case in point. The sequence starts when Thomas reports that he has gotten engaged with a photograph of his and his fiancée's hands, both with new rings (Message 6.6). In reply, he gets two congratulations, both with smiling faces (for reasons of space, only the first one is shown here) (Message 6.7). Jaakko's delighted, empathic congratulation illustrates how the camera makes it possible to integrate facial expressions into responses to convey the reactions prompted by the original message. Getting engaged is a happy occasion. News about it calls forth congratulations and smiles in response.

The second striking practice can be called "format tying," using the format of the responded-to message almost in one-to-one form in the response (see M. Goodwin 1990: 177–188, 92). Thus, messages with faces are responded to with faces, as are torsos with torsos, gestures with gestures, and body parts with similar body parts. The sequence initiated by Thomas's news report continues with a surprising response using such format tying. Instead of congratulating Thomas, Jani sends a tease the next day. From a drinking spree in Tallinn, Estonia, he sent a photograph of his hand with no ring, proudly claiming that no one is going to catch

Message 6.6
Engagement

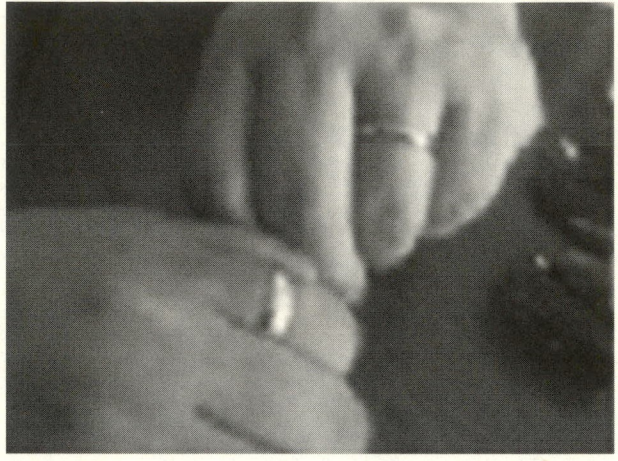

From Thomas 16th July 2002 1:41 p.m.
It took 15 years! But good things come to those who wait.

Message 6.7
Congratulations

From Jarkko: 16.7.18:26 PSD
Congratulations! Jarkko, Leo and Topi

Messages 6.8
Challenge

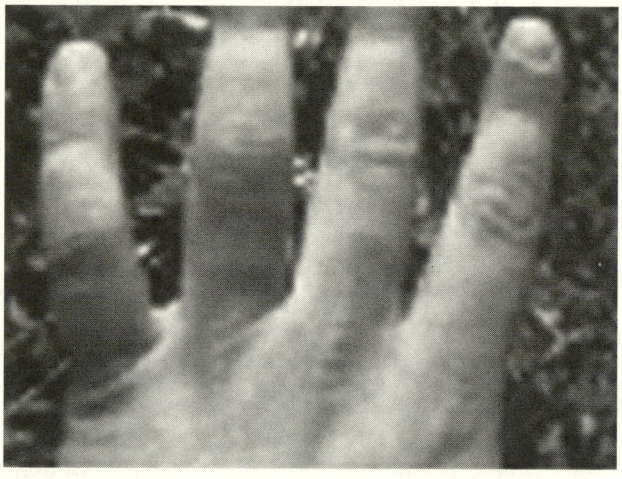

From Jani 17th July 2002 2:11 p.m.
Screw your ring. Nobody snatches me, except miss universe

Message 6.9
Countering the Challenge with an Insult

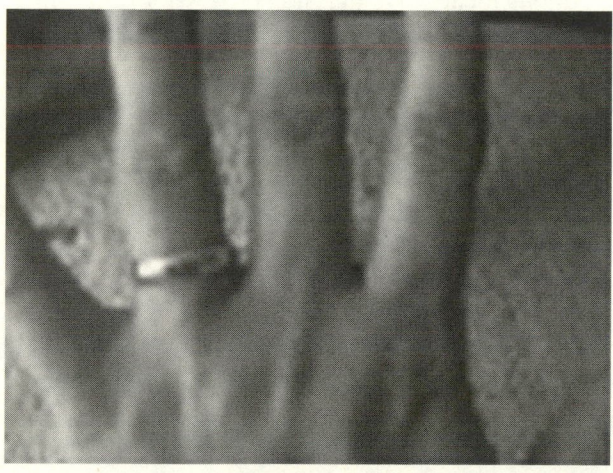

From Thomas 17th July 2002 4:25 p.m.
Well screw you! Just think that I've had more mornings with my
woman than you with both of your hands! Hah hah heh hee

him, except Miss Universe (Message 6.8). However, Thomas does not back down. Instead, he resends a photograph of his ring, turning Jani's bachelor status into an insult (M. Goodwin 1990: 185–188), by suggesting that his marital status provides him with sexual benefits not available to an unmarried young man (Message 6.9).

Bodily responses do not have to be done using the same body part, gesture, or props, but one related to that used in the prior message. For example, in a particularly dirty example, a man sent a photograph of his sexual organ to his girlfriend, who responded with a photograph of her breasts. In another similar, but not sexual instance, one participant took a photograph of his bare bottom—a symbol of contempt—and received a reply of bare thighs and toes, pictured from above a toilet seat.

Conclusions

This Chapter has described various ways in which gestures, faces, and bodies are used as communicative resources in mobile multimedia messages. We have seen that bodies, body parts, and bodies in their environment are put to use in mobile multimedia. For example, they communicate emotive states, reactions to things, and provide a way to use conventional visual symbols methodically. In fact, this is a *striking* feature typical to mobile multimedia messaging. Such means of expression are much less prevalent in mainly textually defined e-mail and text messaging. Among means of expression provided by multimedia phones, the body is a much more important expressive instrument than sound, which was analyzed in the previous Chapter.

Interestingly, the use of body in messaging may be one of the natural "affordances" (see Gibson 1979: 18; Dant 2005: 71–75) of mobile multimedia. With multimedia phones, one can use one's body not just to convey meaning, but also to transmit bodily reactions in messages in comprehensible, conventional form. Thus, although the cameras built into the first multimedia phones were poor in quality, the low quality of imaging did not really matter: people still found uses for it. The body gives a host of surprisingly robust resources for enriching interaction in the wireless domain. These resources are "robust" in the sense that, say, gestures are easy to understand even with fuzzy photographs. When seeing a fuzzy, frozen moment in a still image, recipients are able to imagine the action taking place in the photograph. Lack of movement is not a hindrance to understanding, if the gesture is conventional enough.

Although handset manufacturers are at the moment engaged in an arms race to build increasingly powerful cameras, with new cameras appearing practically every month, this race may be partly off the mark. Similarly, people might simply not want video calls, despite what some industry insiders think (cf. O'Hara et al. 2006). Even in the first generation of multimedia phones, bodies were used in many ways in communication, though fairly few of these uses require video—or benefit from it. The body becomes a resource for interaction with camera phones capable of capturing and sharing still images.

Part III

Mobile Multimedia in Interaction

7

Designing Opening Messages

Part II demonstrated that multimedia phones provide people with a rich means of expression. It is easy to understand that people often keep images in their phones for autobiographic purposes and share images on the screen without sending them. People are able to capture and thus remember significant moments in their lives with their phones. However, people also sometimes send items, turning files on the phone into messages, which is another, equally essential facet of mobile multimedia. The following three chapters examine the issue of multimedia interaction. The question posed in this Chapter is what do people do when they decide not only to keep a photograph or sound file, perhaps for later viewing in their phones, but instead send it to others who are not immediately present? How do they design messages with the recipient in mind?

Using digital cameras typically requires planning: people think ahead and take a camera with them if they believe they will see something interesting and memorable. This is a major difference from "hip top" multimedia devices that follow people everywhere, rendering less photographic and communication-worthy aspects of mundane life communicable in visual and aural form.

However, reporting things with mobile multimedia still requires some planning. Any message makes a claim to the recipient's attention and makes it possible for him or her to analyze the sender, not just the message. Only a few topics—such as photographs of babies, pets, and sights in foreign cities—are inherently interesting, and even these topics may get boring. In contrast, pictures of all-too-familiar streetscapes, workplaces, homes, summer homes, and familiar people are banal and often too boring to carry out any meaningful interaction. In consequence, users have to solve a host of problems in designing multimedia messages. The key problem is how to make the exchange interesting enough to be worth reporting. If one keeps sending uninteresting material, recipients lose interest, get annoyed, and come to define the sender as somehow obsessed with morbid interests (comp. to Bergmann 1993). To avoid such labels, people have to find ways to make their messages interesting enough for recipients with various types of interest arousers (Sacks 1995, II: 12–13, 170–172; also Koskinen et al. 2002: 80–81; Battarbee and Koskinen 2004).

How to Arouse the Recipient's Interest in a Message?

For several reasons, multimedia messaging takes messaging beyond what one finds in photo albums: photographs of familiar streets, workplaces, homes, summer homes, and acquaintances are too banal for meaningful interaction for long, though they nevertheless do provide the main targets of photographing in mobile multimedia (see Okabe and Ito 2004). In an interview conducted in the summer of 2000, we got some clues on how people determine what is suitable for sending with mobile multimedia devices. Mervi, who participated in *Mobile Image* (Koskinen et al. 2002: 41–42), told us about her logic in taking and sending photographs:

> Somehow, I just worry my pictures aren't good enough, and that they should have a point to them. I don't want to send the usual stuff found in photo albums. I'd like to send pictures with an interesting point. But then I worry that if I try something special it won't be understood correctly.

Mervi's answer makes several distinctions that illustrate how mobile images differ from paper snapshots. First, an interesting point is needed to justify an image. Secondly, since mobile phones provide a new technology for photography, images taken and sent with them need to be different from traditional photo albums. Finally, she makes the point that there is a certain risk in sending "interesting" messages: an interesting message may be incomprehensible, difficult to understand, or too odd to be understandable.

How do people try to make their messages interesting enough to be worth sending? To answer this question, we need to look at individual messages to see what kinds of methods people use to guarantee the recipient's interest and to make their messages comprehensible.

News items. Even though most mobile multimedia messages are usually about familiar scenes, this does not mean that they only deal with routines. Even familiar things may be newsworthy (Terasaki 1976; Sacks 1995, II: 218–221; Koskinen 2007a). For instance, we can return to the example of Thomas in Chapter 6, who sent a photograph of two hands, both wearing a new wedding ring. The text explained that it had taken them fifteen years to get to this stage, but it was worth it (Message 6.6). Two recipients congratulated him immediately (Message 6.7). However, with mobile multimedia, news does not need to be about significant events in life. In one message, Markku tells Mari how an older lady had ruffled his hair without any apparent reason. The photograph shows Markku's face and two people in the background. Without text, his message would simply have shown three people in the twilight; the text makes the episode interesting enough to be reportable (Message 7.1).

Dramatization. People may and do take fictive license in dramatizing ordinary things to make them interesting enough to be shared. These dramatizations sometimes borrow story and photograph formats from Hollywood and other media but, more typically, they are designed as commentaries on specific occurrences and relationships among friends. For example, Message 6.2 is a photograph of four young women sitting in the back seat of a car while going to a party. The text says that the (self-proclaimed) "Barbies" are in a taxi. The message focuses on "Patsy's" deep cleavage, which in this context becomes something of an indication

Message 7.1
Markku's Hair

13.7. 23:52 Markku to Leila
What a fixation older ladies have on my hair… The lady in the background
came to ruffle and praise it, and my friend's mother praised it… Help!

Message 7.2
Sunflower

102_0725_0852_08_272Hannato_Anne.psd
Have a sunny afternoon!

Message 7.3
Spiritual Values

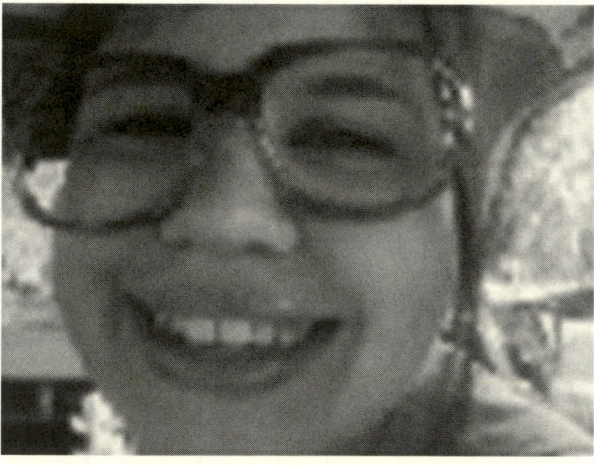

11th July 2002 6:35 p.m. From Liisa
Listen Risto, our spiritual values can be seen in our work and leisure!

Message 7.4
Korso

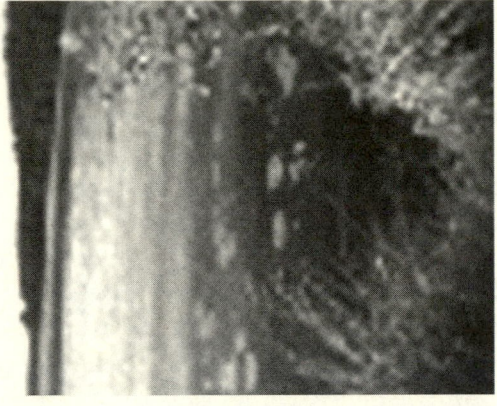

75r12 15.7. 16:08 From Leila to Markku

Oh what a wonder and lovely scene. I know that many people think that nature photos are boring, but I can't but rejoice when you can even find beautiful things in Korso. Another thing: can you do animations and if you can, how?

of her sexual intentions. The message is sent to Markku, who had dated her previously—here the message is designed to make him jealous.

Cheer Ups. Perhaps more than anything else, in everyday use, mobile multimedia is a technology for mutual entertainment. Timo, another informant in *Mobile Image,* had this to say about his experience after using a multimedia device for two months: "This has all been fun and fooling around, kind of communicating experiences and humor" (Koskinen et al. 2002: 77; see also Mäkelä et al. 2000). Such messages designed to bring delight do not have to be informative or intrinsically interesting. Also, these messages are typically easy enough to be understood. Simple messages will do, as the point of these gift-like messages is the gesture of sending the message rather than its content (cf. Taylor and Harper 2002). Another example is designed to cheer up the recipient with a wireless version of a classic method of remembering, sending a bunch of flowers (Message 7.2).

Another prevalent class of cheer up messages consists of several forms of humor. For example, in Message 7.3, Liisa manages to take a particularly funny self-portrait. She is wearing old-fashioned eyeglasses, and her cheeks give her an Oriental look (in truth, she has a narrow face and does not wear glasses). She describes herself to Risto as a yogi or spiritual adviser. He responds with a message in which he congratulates Liisa for sending such a sunny photograph. He also notes that he had laughed for several minutes after seeing the message.

Often humor in messages is far more elaborate. For example, people may build their messages with references to culture and society. The best example of such practice is a case analyzed in more detail in Chapter 12. Participants in the first group of *Mobile Image* utilized characters from *Star Wars I: The Phantom Menace* to tease each other. At the more elaborate end are inside jokes, which may last a long time. The best example of such practice is the "ladies' man culture" developed by the male group in *Mobile Image*. Participants in that group made a habit of photographing practically every young woman they met, and sending these photographs to other group members with text suggesting that these women were their latest sexual conquests. They knew these women in real life, and knew that these ladies' man messages were a hoax. Still, the joke went on for several weeks until it grew old (see Koskinen et al. 2002: 85–90).

Saving Bad Pictures: Art and Accounts. A rare and somewhat curious way to make photographs interesting is to label them "works of art." These messages are not useful or intrinsically interesting in any obvious way. Rather, aesthetic qualities become the reasons for sending them. With this label, people typically "saved" incomprehensible, but beautiful pictures: once one labels something "art," one can send meaningless, mysterious, and even insulting pictures. These messages typically reported beautiful light effects, but also subjects such as fish, cups of coffee, and all-too-familiar scenes from one's home street (see Koskinen et al. 2002: 69–71). This practice plays on how the lay public perceives modern art, first by turning a commonplace object into a work of art, and second, by making use of modern artists' habits of explaining their work in mystical terms.

Another way to save pictures is to account for sending them. In Message 7.4, Leila sends a photograph from Korso, a poorly regarded neighborhood in suburban Helsinki. What makes the scene worth reporting is that she is enthralled with the unexpected beauty of the scene. This message illustrates another, though rare, practice used to "save" messages. Although Leila thinks the message will be boring for some recipients, her excuse for sending the message is that she found the scene beautiful. With accounts like these, people are able to send photographs that look uninteresting at first glance.

Messages without Interest Arousers

Although in general people try to secure the recipient's interest in their messages with the means analyzed above, at least two types of messages form an exception to this rule. Some things are defined as interesting enough to be shared following the conventions of the Kodak culture (Chalfen 1987). Another exception is messages that maintain visual co-presence (Ito 2005). As Ito has observed, they mostly take place between couples. However, as the following analysis shows, these messages can be found in other situations and relationships as well.

Kodak Culture on the Phone

Some topics are practically always legitimate enough to be shared in the sense that they can be sent at will without any attempt to arouse the recipient's interest in them. These topics consist mostly of things typical of the Kodak culture, such as travel photos and pictures of babies and pets. Take the example of travel photographs from exotic places. A colleague based in San Francisco once told me how he had a few weeks earlier taken photographs with his mobile phone in Tokyo, and sent them to his wife. She had responded with text messages, instructing him to take more photographs of certain places. Mobile phones enabled these people to coordinate their vision across the Pacific (fieldnote, March 2, 2004). We have already seen examples of messages of this type. The very first example in this book, Postcard from Greece, was in a greeting card format.

Other intrinsically interesting categories of messages are the actions, moods, or sayings of friends and acquaintances, babies, pets, and "trophies" like cars and photographs of the family. Of course, the recipients' interest in these photos cannot be taken for granted, though they are expected to show interest in them. It would be curious not to get an admiring response to an audio message containing a picture of a baby. Still, the recipient's interest is not automatic. For example, if a message is too banal, or if it is sent several times, it may arouse requests to stop messaging. As a case analyzed by Battarbee and Koskinen (2004) shows, recipients may even get bored with messages of babies and toddlers. There can be too much of a good thing.

Maintaining Visual Co-Presence

In some cases, messages are sent without interest arousers, and they are about things deemed trivial even in the Kodak culture. After analyzing the messaging of two young couples, Ito (2005) pointed out that there are people who send messages in which the content is essentially banal, but the senders do not even try to justify their messages in any way. Especially couples in a romantic relationship "were more likely to post very mundane photos that conveyed ambient visual information rather than explicit communication.... These photos...resemble the ongoing lightweight co-presence that we found couples maintaining via the exchange of text sweet nothings" (Ito 2005).

By sending these messages, people show that they are thinking of the other person. This is certainly the case in some of the data. For instance, in Message 7.5, Jani sends photographs from the summer cottage to his girlfriend without any text whatsoever—without, that is, any attempt to justify these messages.

Similar situations exist as well. The first situation is flirting, a special case in an intimate relationship. Secondly, friends could send photographs

Message 7.5
((No subject))

080_0716_1223_12_336 Jani to Susanna.jpg

of practically anything. Even in our first study, *Mobile Image*, friends made messages out of a whole range of images, including old socks, tabletops, soda bottles, and ads familiar to everyone. Typically, these photographs were sent from trips or from meetings and conferences that proved to be boring. This kind of messaging could continue for several messages before the recipients began to suggest that enough is enough. The third case relates to new phones and neophytes to mobile multimedia messaging. When people acquired a multimedia phone for the first time, they typically sent photographs of almost anything to people that they knew with a multimedia phone. In that case, of course, the justification for messages was obvious: experimentation, a need to get confirmation that the system works, and also notifying the recipient that one is accessible with this media.

Thus, although Ito's observation about couples maintaining visual co-presence holds, her conclusions are somewhat problematic due to her limited data. Most significantly, these presence-maintaining messages are limited not only to couples with romantic relationships. They also take place in several other relationships and situations too. More typically, such messages are restricted to experimentation with newly acquired phones.

Response Instructions

Multimedia messages are not always construed as self-standing postcard-like messages that do not require a reply (though make a reply possible). Often, they are built to elicit a response from the recipient. A number of means can be used to shape multimedia messages into starting points for interaction.

In their simplest form, response instructions utilize what conversation analysts call "adjacency pairs": actions like questions and answers that come in pairs, with little delay, and are performed by two different people (for a succinct statement, see Schegloff and Sacks 1973). If the "second part" of the pair is not produced, the sender can hold the recipient accountable for his or her reproach, and ultimately demand an explanation. For example, in Message 7.6, Tiina sends a photograph of a glass of wine to Thomas. In text, she first greets him, and continues with a riddle asking what is in the travelers' glasses. In Message 7.7, Thomas first guessed ("Red wine"), thus treating the message as a riddle. In audio, he sang a jingle from a well-known TV advertisement selling juice concentrate for children, transforming the response into a joke.

Message 7.6
What's in the Glass?

Text: From Tiina to Thomas.
Greetings from the Silja pub. A riddle: what's in the travellers' glasses? Have a nice Sunday!
Audio file: ((Background noise from restaurant; background music: Who'll Stop
the Rain)) Female voice: And the artist of the night, Jari Mäki. Here's a sample

Message 7.7
What's in the Glass, Response

Text: Thomas to Tiina.
Our guess is red wine, but we could not make sense of the sound.
Audio file:
((Male voice, sings, my translation)):
Always drink Juice Cat, it always tastes great, Juice Cat

Of course, not all response instructions exploit normative expectations typical to adjacency pairs. For example, love messages and gossip openings are usually built to elicit a response. However, with a response, the recipient potentially implicates himself in something undesirable, especially in the case of gossiping, a "morally contaminated" activity (Bergmann 1993). For instance, in one case, Markku sends greetings from his younger brother and his girlfriend, reporting their plans to move to the town of Rauma. However, he also reports that his brother plans neither to work nor to study in his new hometown even though he does not know anyone there. He closes the message with an evaluative tag component (Message 7.8).

Message 7.8
Markku to Mari

Greetings from Ike and Berit. They're moving to Rauma in August, when Berit is starting business school. Ike plans to have free time, he won't work, and doesn't plan to study either... sounds BAD. He doesn't even know anyone in Rauma... Uh huh huh, nothing good is going to come of this...

This is a classic gossip opening, which uses an innocent piece of news to get recipients involved in gossiping. Markku received two replies, one from Mari five hours later, and another from Liisa three and a half hours after Mari's reply. Mari suggested that living in a new place will remove Ike's illusions about work and living as a couple, and Liisa sent Markku an idiom which says that life will soften even the hardest block of wood (free translation by IK). They thus acknowledged Markku's message, but with the five-hour delay and these idioms indirectly suggested that they were not interested in pursuing this topic. Markku got the point (for idioms, see Drew and Holt 1988).

Placing Multimedia Elements in Messages

When analyzing messages in terms of how they prepare subsequent action, we need to pay attention to one more item, the placement and order of multimedia elements in messages. Whether response instructions are relevant for the future course of action or not depends partly on where they appear. In particular, at the end of the message, they acquire a prominent status in the recipient's mind. Thus, in the Korso scenery example earlier in this Chapter (Message 7.4), there was a question about making animations at the end of the message. The question was unrelated to the rest of the message, but still prompted a long and immediate reply.

If we look again at the gossip opening in Message 7.8, and map the order of Markku's message, we see how it started with greetings from Ike and Berit, and continued with their plans to move out of town. Then Markku first went on to describe Ike's plans to have good time in Rauma, and second to evaluate these plans. Should Markku have opened the message with the description and evaluation of Ike's plans, this would have been an obvious attempt to open gossip. When the message is designed as Markku does it, the message may be taken as a news item, not necessarily a gossip opening with morally questionable overtones. Also, the evaluation is grounded in facts when he enters into it at the end of his message. Finally, the evaluative item—which gives the recipients the possibility to be evaluative too, and thus open gossip—is placed at the end of the message. In this position, it typically becomes the starting point for the next action.

Even if messages have response instructions that, in normal cases, would direct responses in a certain direction, they may be placed in messages such that recipients find it more relevant to bypass them and design their response on another item. If they respond to messages that do several actions at once, they may also choose which parts of the message they respond to, or respond to several items in the message. The point is that complex messages provide several alternative courses of action for the recipient, and response depends at least partly on how items in these complex messages are ordered.

Conclusions

With mobile multimedia devices, people are able to capture things, events, feelings, and memories, and bring them to the recipients' attention. Potentially, mobile multimedia is a powerful instrument for observing and reporting everyday life. However, there are social limits to what kinds of messages are sent. Any multimedia message makes a claim on the recipient's attention. To make messages interesting enough for recipients, they ought to differ from traditional snapshots, and be interesting enough to be worth sending while still being intelligible (see Battarbee and Koskinen 2004; Koskinen et al. 2002: 41–42).

As we have seen, people take care of these requirements through several means. Most typically, people may present the things they report as somehow newsworthy, and they may dramatize them to make them interesting. Even incomprehensible images can be sent if they can be described as having "artistic" qualities. Often, messages are designed to cheer up the recipient. With methods like these, people manage the commonness that inevitably threatens to make multimedia messages boring and banal (Koskinen 2007a). Simultaneously, they ensure that messages are intelligible, for example, by making sure that things in photographs are identifiable and meaningful. Finally, senders may also exploit normative conventions typical to conversation with response instructions of various sorts ranging from what conversation analysts call "adjacency pairs" (Schegloff and Sacks 1973) to gossip openings (Bergmann 1993).

We have seen that multimedia messages are complex constructions. When designing their messages with an eye on the recipient, senders have multiple means at their disposal. It is next up to the recipient to make sense of the message, analyze why it was sent in the first place, and to decide whether it requires a reply of some sort. The following Chapter turns to what recipients do with mobile multimedia messages.

8

Replies, Responses, and Gestalt Modifications

What distinguishes mobile multimedia from traditional media is its interactivity. While some messages are just received and not responded to, this is not always the case. When a message arrives in the recipient's mobile phone, it requires attention, sensemaking, analysis, and may possibly require a reply. These activities take the recipient away from his previous line of activity for a moment. This Chapter studies the main types of responses and relates them to the preceding messages.

In rough terms, several things happen when a new message arrives. First, the recipient has to read the text, see the image, and hear the possible sound file in order to make sense of the message. He or she may also venture deeper into the interpretation, for example, to identify people, places, and activities in the message, in addition, to checking whether a response is needed or not, and if it is needed, what kind of response is appropriate. Only after this work, can the recipient start to design a response. Even in a relatively simple case of, say, greetings, the response is not necessarily easy to deliver. The recipient must decide the format (for example, sound or text), choose wording, find or shoot a suitable picture, and coordinate all multimedia elements into a coherent message. All this work necessarily takes place before sending the message. Finally, he or she needs to decide whether an immediate response is required, or whether it is better to delay the message. Reasons for delaying the message can range from legal (driving a car) to situational (stopping a meeting for sending a multimedia message).

Consequently, in deciding whether to reply, the recipient has to use several kinds of analyses. Depending on the situation, the sender, and the content of the message, he or she has several options. However, to arrive at a decision about what to do, the recipient has to open and study the message to see whether it is witty, silly, or important enough to require an immediate response, and to see whether it contains response instructions or not. It is only then that the next task, designing a reply, can start.

Recipient-Initiated Action

If no response instructions are given, it is up to the recipient to decide whether and how to reply. For example, I did not answer the "Postcard from Greece" analyzed in Chapter 1. Such a message may justify a "thank you" message in response, but does not require one. We seldom reply to postcards anyway—or if we do, it is *in passim* months later. This is also the case with other types of messages, including simple documents of mundane, fairly trivial items, photographs of pets, jokes, and artsy pieces. These messages can be responded to, but nothing in them require a response. In fact, many multimedia messages remains unanswered, making messaging into monologue-like, one-way communication (see Koskinen et al. 2002; Koskinen and Kurvinen 2002; for similar construction in text messages, see Laursen 2006: 64-68).

Yet some of these messages are responded to for several reasons. Sometimes significant content prompts response, which is typically the case with photographs of pets and babies. Sometimes the message is so witty, beautiful, interesting, or deserving in other ways that it deserves a compliment, or perhaps some other kind of reply.

Message 8.1 shows how some of these reasons may be at work simultaneously. Message 8.1 is a response to Markku's travel story that documented his holiday trip to the town of Vaasa, located about 400 kilometers northwest of Helsinki. Markku sent a series of seven messages in which he reported on his trip from Helsinki to Vaasa and back. One incident was particularly special. When he had been out one night dancing, an older lady had come to ruffle and compliment his hair (Message 7.1). In response to this travel story, Leila sent a photograph of a lake and a text that displays her reactions to these messages in several ways, beginning with a "thank you," a commentary on the bunnies photographed by Markku, and an empathic assessment (Goodwin and Goodwin 1987; Kurvinen 2003) of a funny incident on his trip.

However, some responses are based on another kind of recipient analysis. Messages may be incomprehensible enough to warrant a need for specification. They may also be ridiculous and laughable enough to warrant a tease as a reply, as I will show later in this Chapter. Sometimes responses build on the fact that the earlier message was somehow outrageous, distasteful, or raunchy. In all these cases, typical responses target not only the message, but also the sender, labeling him as deviant, as we shall later see in Messages 9.2–9.5.

Message 8.1
Country Life at Its Best

Leila to Markku
Country life at its best. Thanks for the messages, bunnies still seem to be alive. Your hair is a funny thing. I don't know what I'd do if middle-aged men ruffled my hair...

Replies

In some ways, things are easier for the recipient when a message contains response instructions. They show the recipient that a reply is expected. They also include instructions about the proper reply. Thus, a question is a typical response instruction: a proper reply to a question is an answer. Similarly, a proper reply to a greeting is a return greeting (Heritage 1989), to a request a response, to an assessment another assessment (Goodwin and Goodwin 1987), and to an invitation either an acceptance or a rejection (Pomerantz 1984). In all these cases, convention requires a proper reply: people are held accountable for replying in the proper fashion, or they are rude and reprimanded. Reprimands range from reinstating the question or the greeting to accusations of being rude and inconsiderate. Following Goffman, these acts are here called replies (Goffman 1981: 35).

Messages 8.2
Prize
((No picture))

Hi! Does anyone have good pictures from yesterday? For example, at least 100 pictures were taken with Tony's camera. Does anyone have a picture of me with the trophy? J

Message 8.3
Prize, Response

It's easy to smile when you win. Lunch companion is available near the School of Business. E

Messages 8.2–8.3 provide an example of a reply. In Message 8.2, "J" requests his friends to send him a photograph. On the previous day, he had been in a floor ball tournament (floor ball is a form of indoor hockey), which his team had won. He knew that his friends had been at the tournament and had been taking photographs all along. He asks to get a photograph of the trophy, which is granted to him in Message 8.3 by "E."

Replies do not necessarily lead only to individual messages that close the sequence. Sometimes replies are much more elaborate. For example, a tease typically proceeds in three phases (Drew 1987). First, there is a message that contains something ridiculous or something laughable. This message is followed by a tease, which formulates the prior message as laughable, and makes a challenge to the sender of the original message. The tease is followed by a "receipt" by the teased person, who, typically, is a good sport. If not, his serious action presents a challenge to the teaser, who then has to decide whether to back up or let the sequence escalate, possibly leading to an open confrontation. Anyone familiar with teasing can expose himself to teasing by, say, presenting an exaggerated and silly opinion that calls forth a tease, which can then be responded to in the third slot that follows the tease.

Riddles are an example of an activity that has at least three parts. In sending a riddle, the sender not only elicits a response, but also gets a chance to continue the riddle, or to compliment the recipient for a good guess in receipt.

However, riddles are often more complicated. In particular, people can extend riddles by providing a difficult riddle and then a series of increasingly accurate clues, when the first guesses are wrong. This took place in the first riddle of *Mobile Image*. On Friday, September 3, 1999, Tony sent a picture of a café to his colleagues in Helsinki with a subject line of "picture riddle" (Message 8.4). In the course of the following two hours, he provided several pictures as tips to the recipients. The ninth message of the series (Message 8.5) produced the final tip, a steel construction of some sort standing behind Tony. The tenth message (Message 8.6) finally provided the answer by showing his face next to the Eiffel Tower. In this message, he finally explains that he is currently in Paris visiting his cousin, adding other news about his trip. This series also makes the joke about the Giant Green Sociologist in Chapter 3 understandable: that photo is based on Tony's habit of photographing himself in front of tourist attractions.

Riddles may also call forth responses from several people, who come to coordinate their line of action for a moment in search of the right answer. In one series in *Radiolinja*, there was an unclear picture of a furry and pink thing, and the text "Picture puzzle." After Erik had thus set up the puzzle, he received two responses, first from Jari, who guessed "a dog's belly," adding a picture of hard-thinking Donald Duck to show how much trouble he had gone through in thinking about the right answer.

Messages 8.4
The Paris Puzzle: Opening

Date: Fri, 3 Sep 1999 15:12 Subject: Picture puzzle

Message 8.5
The Paris Puzzle: A Hint

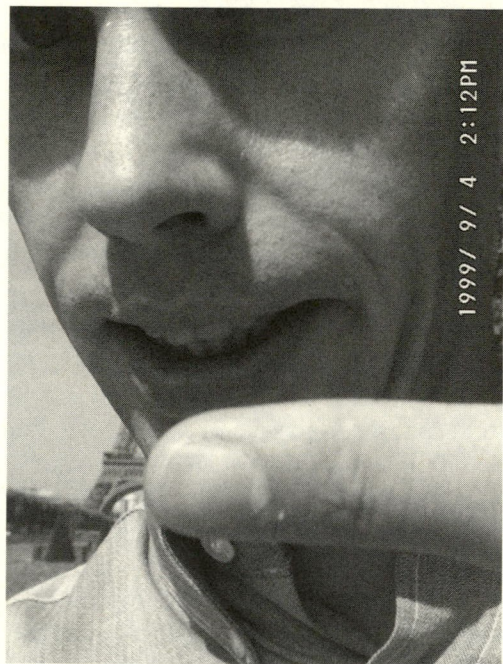

Date: Sun, 5 Sep 1999 17:04
(From Tony to all)
Subject: Picture puzzle 9
Where is he now? The last
tip is right behind me.

Message 8.6
The Paris Puzzle: The Answer

Date: Sun, 5 Sep 1999 17:10 (From Tony to all)
Subject: Picture puzzle 10
Ehm, in Paris of course, visiting my cousin. The Communicator has deservedly aroused interest in cafés. The usually—so—reserved bigcityfrench talk to me like I'm a dog owner or the mother of a small child. See you on Tuesday, t

Sami then admitted that he had no idea, but proceeded with a wild guess saying that a dog is involved. The riddle is over when Erik provides the right answer: the original picture was "The bottom of our dog (a--). Did you get it?" Riddles may thus become collective things.

Responses can also take other forms, such as when they lead to documenting places (see Ling and Julsrud 2005). One particularly interesting sequence is too long to be reported here in detail, but the following outline gives a picture of what happened.

The sequence starts when Anna-Maija sends her after sauna greetings to Kira. A response from Emma comes seven minutes later. In the response, two girls are hugging and smiling into the camera, replying to Anna-Maija not only in words, but also through bodily gestures. However, in their response, the girls also ask to see the sauna cabin and the lake, requiring at least two messages to reply properly. Next Anna-Maija follows this instruction literally. Her first reply shows the sauna cabin, and the next reply is about the lake.

By now, her response has not only fulfilled Kira's, Piitu's, and Emma's wishes to see these items, but provided these items in perfect order as well. However, although these two messages would have provided a sufficient reply to the girls, Anna-Maija does not stop here. On the contrary, she continues to document a host of other items in her summer place. In addition to the sauna and the lake, she sends pictures of the outdoor "kitchen," a barbecue place built on the rock; the well; the sleeping cabin; "the whole"; the boat; the jetty and the dog; and a picture of her mother preparing food.

Perhaps this extended reply was elicited by Kira's, Piitu's and Emma's original message. Had they asked for only one picture, she would not have gone on such a photographing spree. In any case, there seems to be something like the *et cetera* principle (Garfinkel 1967) at work here. Anna-Maija treats the girls' request not just literally, but as a request for providing complete visual documentation of her summer place (see Ling and Julsrud 2005).

Anna-Maija's extended reply illustrates how even fairly simple joint activities such as answers to requests may provide a starting point for many types of more complicated activities. First, the sequence shows that mobile multimedia messages make heavy use of verbal and pictorial resources as well as bodily resources. The girls' request contains a reply to Anna-Maija's greetings in the form of "hugs," which is a conventional greeting form among girls in Helsinki. Secondly, the girls' message shows that multimedia is a social technology: at least three people saw Anna-Maija's greeting and together created a response to it together (see Relieu 2002; Weilenmann and Larsson 2001; Kasesniemi 2003).

Responses

As the previous example suggests, recipients sometimes go beyond the boundaries suggested in the response instructions given in a message; they respond not only to items requested, but also to something else in the prior message. As Goffman (1981: 35) argues, this something else may consist of a failed item in communication. As he notes, sometimes the recipient "abstracts from the sender's statement merely its qualifications as something to be heard and understood. It is to the situation of failed communication, not to what is being communicated, that the recipient reacts." Goffman continues: "To call these signals "replies" seems a little inappropriate, for in the closest sense, they do not constitute a reply to what was said; the term 'response' seems better." (Goffman 1981: 35).

In mobile multimedia, recipients typically "respect" the instructions they receive from the sender. However, recipients may go beyond the frame provided by the sender to initiate action on their own. Perhaps the most typical conventional response consistes of identification requests that take place when there are unknown people or other unclear elements in the picture. Senders typically respond to these identification requests by providing a response that clarifies the obscurity.

In the following example, Markku had sent several messages to Leila (they are analyzed later in Messages 9.7–9.9). In the final message of this series, he writes about his plans and the weather, but also mentions the name "Kauko." This Kauko, according to Markku, is playing and apparently talking about a boy who is looking for something. The next afternoon, Leila returns to the topic of Kauko, asking who he is (Message 8.8). She adds a picture of their mutual friend Anne to the message, turning Anne into a professor in text, apparently because with her glasses and inquisitive look she has the look of a scholar in the popular imagination. In this jocular message, this trick still manages to add to the compulsive power of Leila's inquiry. Professors are teachers, and as teachers they have a right to pose questions and a right to expect answers promptly. And Markku answers, including an image from the cover of a CD which shows that Kauko is a local rock singer. With Kauko's easily recognizable face, the image provides clear enough identification for Leila. He also adds a few lines from one of Kauko's song to the message, giving it a poetic quality (Message 8.9).

Note how Leila's identification request is not in any way called forth by Markku's previous message, although this message makes Leila's request possible. Instead, it was an independent act, a response in Goffmanian terminology. Identification requests like Leila's are typical when unknown people or references to unknown people appear in multimedia messages. Often, these requests have a jocular overtone, like in Message 8.8. Still, they are treated as serious requests in interactional terms: responses to identification requests are typically identifications, which guarantees that all parties to the interaction know its referents.

Gestalt Modifications

Some responses are still more unconventional than Leila's query in Message 8.8. Sometimes nothing in the original message can anticipate the response, and there is little if any coherence between the response and the previous message. Most novelties in mobile multimedia messaging are based on modifying gestalt contextures (comp. Gurwitsch 1964:

Message 8.7
Good Nights

Markku to Leila

There are plants as well. It's really hot – I have to sleep on the floor. Kauko's playing; seek, boy, seek. Sometimes life is like dream. G'night.

Message 8.8
Who is Kauko?

Leila to Markku

Prof asks again: who is Kauko?

Message 8.9
Who is Kauko, Response

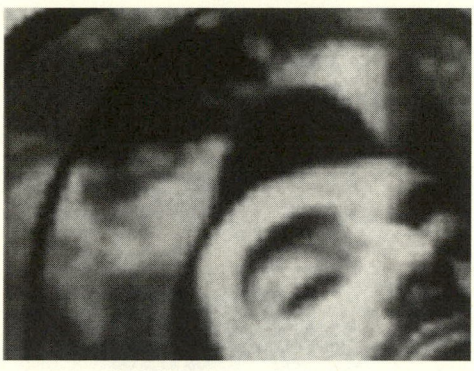

Markku to Leila
Today kauko plays: "girl, you're a star, and you still glow, still glow. Boy, you are a star and glow like a star." PS. The facial expression in Cabbage's face was fairly tight... keep your windows open :)

134–136, 217). We saw an instance of such a switch in Chapter 3, in which we encountered the Giant Green Sociologist. In that example, the receipient turned the original, postcard-like message into a horror scene in which the giant threatened the city by manipulating the image and adding new text. The response used the original image, which, however, took on a totally new meaning.

As also mentioned in Chapter 3, the pilot group of *Mobile Image* created a lively image manipulation culture that was put in the service of joking. Some of these modifications of gestalt contextures were achieved by simply placing photographs in new contexts, while most used image manipulations of some sort in combination with such recontextualization. In Messages 8.10–8.11, the pilot group's members had just received a package of T-shirts imprinted with their research group's name. Message 8.10 shows one member of the group wearing the shirt and posing in typical fashion photography style. The text explains how the group's trendy spring collection has just arrived, which places the message in the world of fashion advertising. Message 8.11 elaborates on the joke with picture manipulation, again in the style of fashion photography, and by including a more elaborate text creating an imaginary conversation between the two characters in the ad.

Message 8.10
Spring Collection Erik

The Smart Products Spring Collection offers you trendy, timeless clothing for spring.

Message 8.11
Fashion News Simon

— Who's that fashionable dandy with that fab T-shirt? So cool it makes me hot!— Hey babe, I'll be in Paris in June, interested in a sip of Dom P. at my place? By the way, I have a Ph.D. in sociology.

Gestalt contextures may be altered even more dramatically. As the following two messages show, responses can reinterpret the preceding message in a radically new way, usually in the service of humor. Message 8.12 is one of the first visual innovations in *Mobile Image*. In this message, Erik explains the technology being used in the study. The pilot group had access to an experimental server hosted by one of Nokia's research centers. In his message, Erik explains how these servers function and gives their addresses. In doing so, he complains about bugs in it (adding a picture of a bug), and then details which programs can be used to access the site. At the end of the message, he does an atypical closing. Instead of a greeting and textual signature, he includes a picture of himself, in which he appears wearing a summer shirt and sunglasses. On the surface, this message delivers important technical information, and is not designed to require a reply of any kind. And if it would call for a reply, the expected response would be a query concerning technical details, or a response to Erik's somewhat coy request to get help testing the site with Pine (a mail program used in UNIX).

Simon's response in Message 8.13 is anything but expected. Instead of asking about technical details or telling about his experiences with the system, he picked up the last item in the message, Erik's self-portrait, and turns it into a joke about the former president of the country, Urho Kekkonen. This joke builds on the suposed resemblance between Erik and Mr. Kekkonen, both bald men who wear glasses. Everything else, however, is changed. Erik's technical message was turned into a joke. His face represents someone else's. The context has changed from some unnamed outdoor place to Red Square, apparently a comment on Mr. Kekkonen's frequent habit of building his foreign policy on good relations with the Soviet Union. Erik was given a suit and tie, his glasses were made bigger in the Kekkonen style, and a flag was added to the background to create an aura of formality.

Though Erik's original message was organized as a "for your information" report aiming to provide the others with critical technical information about how to manage network connections, Simon's response radically modified the message, keeping only two elements, but organizing them into a completely new gestalt contexture (Gurwitsch 1964). Modifications like these take place occasionally, often leading to barely more than momentary fun. However, as Chapter 12 will show, some of these modifications may lead to more stable changes in messaging.

Message 8.12
Server Erik

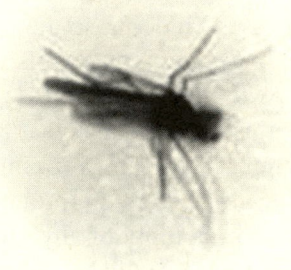

Subject: server
Hi...
For your information, the mobile album of group 1 is at: http://ncc1.pictlan19.cellular-data.com/test99/ there are several bugs in it, but you get the idea

Pictures are sent to:test195@[195.195.195.95]It may be that this only works with the Communicator's mail program. I was told that it doesn't work with Outlook, and apparently not with Netscape either. Would anyone like to try pine?? This is only for private use, but I'll try to make it public so that we could share messages with others.... back soon....Best wishes:

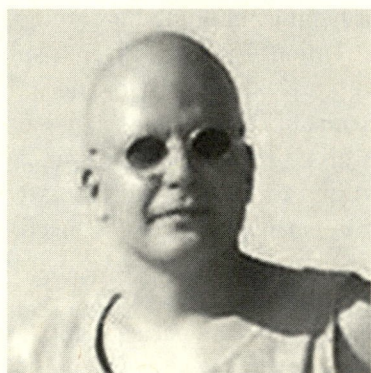

Message 8.13
Served (My Country) Simon

Re: served (my country) The speech of the President of Republic Urho Kekkonen on Red Square was received with enthusiasm. The President stressed the importance of good neighbor relations with Northern Europe

Conclusions: Recipient Actions as Interpretations of Multimedia Messages

This Chapter has shown how mobile multimedia messages create a situation in which the recipient must not only analyze the message, but must also think about whether a reply is needed. Multimedia messaging is an interactive sport, though not every message elicits a response. However, a close analysis of recipient action shows that there are good reasons for recipient action, whatever it turns out to be. This Chapter has shown that when they receive messages, people get engaged in many kinds of activities. When we see their replies and responses, we have access to some of this interpretive and constructive work.

Recipient activity can be classified into a few main types depending on its relationship to the previous message. When no response instructions exist, a typical response shows that the previous message was interesting enough to deserve a reply, and also indicates the reason for this appreciation. These reasons range from the beauty of the picture and sense of shock felt when one sees the original message to the hard work that has gone into the original message. The case of replies is simpler in terms of interaction: not responding to, say, a question would be noticeable, and would even be seen as offensive behavior. Questions typically prompt replies, much like in conversation (Schegloff and Sacks 1973). In responses (Goffman 1981), the recipient gets outside the frame elicited in the previous message. Some responses maintain referents in the earlier message. Some responses are considerably more surprising, taking their elements from previous messages, but modifying them into a new gestalt. Typically, these responses take action away from its previous line; thus, instead of speaking about responses, we reserve a new term for them, gestalt modification (comp. Gurwitsch 1964: 134–136).

In comparative terms, multimedia messages seldom lead to long exchanges in the same manner as text messages. Kasesniemi (2003: 159–215) and Laursen (2005) have described how text messages often get organized into a long series of actions and responses. Laursen even describes text messaging in terms of an A-B-A-B formula in which two people exchange messages over a span of several messages. In contrast, with the possible exception of some intimate messages (see Okabe and Ito 2006) and travelogues, multimedia messages seldom lead to long exchanges like these. Rather, multimedia messages are creations of the moment, amusing recipients only for brief periods of time.

9

How People Stop Messaging

An episode of interaction with mobile multimedia is typically over when the sequences analyzed in Chapter 8 come to an end. Although it is possible to continue an answer with, say, a thank you message, there is no need to do that. Similarly, when the correct answer to a riddle has been given, there is no need to continue that interaction. Interaction halts naturally at this closing point.

When there is no such natural closing point, messaging might still continue for a long time (comp. to text messages in Laursen 2005: esp. 54–56, 64–65), and become boring as well as annoying. In this situation, the recipients have a problem. They would like to stop messaging, but this is not as simple as it would seem. A declining response may prompt problems in subsequent interaction. For example, the sender may become embarrassed or hurt, and may even lose face (Gross and Stone 1964; Goffman 1967: 5–45). The more likely people are to meet again, the more they will try to keep the interaction going and help everyone maintain face. In conversational analytic terms, there is a preference organization at work. For instance, an invitation elicits acceptance as the preferred response turn. Turning the invitation down is a dispreferred turn. Preferred turns are typically given directly, with no delay; hesitations, hedges, or justifications are typical of dispreferred turns (see Pomerantz 1984).

Most responses in multimedia follow this logic. However, for a number of reasons, experiences offered for popular consumption may also be rejected, downplayed or made fun of. A certain banality is almost built into MMS, which focuses on mundane experiences rather than, say, the key rituals of life, or experiences with fine art. This banality may go overboard, and lose the recipient's interest. Also, the report may sometimes stretch the bounds of what is morally acceptable—for example, by being sexually explicit (see Kurvinen 2003; for text messages, see Laursen 2005: 59–60). Recipients, then, may have many different reasons for interrupting or redirecting the messaging, even when it may be difficult to do so without insulting the sender. How can they accomplish closings without causing the sender to lose face?

Extraneous Breaking Points and Conventional Symbols for Closures

Even though multimedia messages as such may continue for several turns, there is at least one natural closing point that works systematically: nighttime. An exchange that takes place in the evening does not normally continue the next day. The night is not just a natural closing point, but is sometimes also marked as such symbolically with good night messages that are particularly effectively in stopping messaging (see Laursen 2006: 67-68). Of course, this is what they are designed to do in ordinary life as well. Most people learn in childhood that "good night" means that it is time to quiet down and go to bed, which means restraining further attempts to maintain conversation or other forms of interaction. Such messages close messaging resolutely, but politely and, among family at least, often with an affectionate content, as in Message 9.1.

Of course, there are exceptions to this practice. For one, messaging can continue the next morning on the same topic, but it has to be rein-stalled with a message that re-introduces it. In *Radiolinja*, Tom had a habit of sending the same good morning message every morning from

Message 9.1
((No subject))

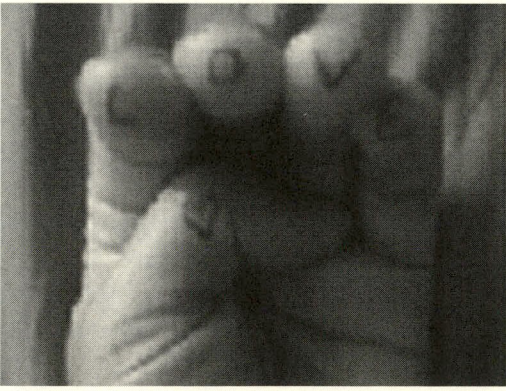

Laila to Thomas
Good night my darling, my love! My fingers are singing... The love of my life!!

his workplace, which opened exchange on the same topic every morning. Another exception to the general rule that message sequences end at night is when messages from the previous day are responded to in the morning, but with apologies. Thus, when questions that arrive in the evening are not answered for some reason (going to bed early), people may reply in the morning, adding an explanation that they went to bed early, or did not see the message for some other reason.

Multimedia messages also provide visual means for closing ongoing activities using conventional symbols. Kurvinen, Battarbee, and Koskinen (2006) have described a case in which a wife sent a good morning greeting to her husband, including a photograph of her still sleepy face. The husband forwarded this photograph to several friends as a mock personal ad. She responded to those recipients by sending a counter-tease about her husband. She sent her husband, however, a photograph of excrement in a baby's diaper, building on a conventional Finnish proverbial expression of contempt without actually saying the four-letter word. He got the message and stopped recycling the tease for a few days.

Status Degradation

Garfinkel (1956) defined "status degradation" as "communicative work between persons, whereby the public identity of an actor is transformed into something looked on as lower in the local scheme of social types." Under normal circumstances, people categorize others, expect certain behaviors and opinions from them, and grant them certain rights and duties. Degrading a person makes the community's values salient by insulting the perpetrator, and shows that should he continue the line of action that justified the degradation in the first place, others may treat him in a less respectful fashion in the future. Any parent knows that an efficient way to get a small child to behave better is to call him a "baby" (Sacks 1972a, 1972b).

In mobile multimedia, status degradation ceremonies are simpler than those analyzed by Garfinkel, but still happen. Sometimes they are based on labeling the perpetrator with terms that suggest that something in his behavior is wrong. Kurvinen (2007) has described an instance from the early days of mobile multimedia. In September 1999, Erik was in a conference in Hvitträsk, a former villa of the famous Art Nouveau architect Eliel Saarinen, situated 30 kilometers outside Helsinki. He reported his experience with a string of forty photographs. His report began with photographs of people (presenters) and their activities (talks), but soon continued to less obvious topics such as food, the Web, and finally his own socks.

This contour was quickly noticed in responses, as we can see in the following four textual responses to Erik's string of photographs. First, after five of Erik's photographs, Kaisa sends a response in which she wonders whether Erik is bored (Message 9.2). After 4:00 pm, Erik sends two photographs—salad and a pastry—from a lunch break, prompting a reply from Kai labeling him "crazy" (Message 9.3.), which is followed a minute later by a still stronger—and food-related —formulation of "photo diarrhea" by Kaisa (Message 9.4). The next day, Simon finally asks what on earth they are doing at the conference (Message 9.5).

Message 9.2. *Subject: Coffee and Bubble Gum* 1.9.1999 3:37 (Kaisa to all) ((no image))Hi. Is it that boring out there? Or really fun? Erik, are you listening to the conference at all?

Message 9.3. *Re: Danish* 1.9.1999 6:14 (Kai to all) ((no image))Erik has gone crazy. Thanks Erik for documenting the food carefully for all of us.Kai

Message 9.4. *RE: Danish Photo Diarrhea* 1.9.1999 6:13 (From Kaisa) ((no image))Erik has a helluva PHOTO DIARRHEA

Message 9.5. *Posters* 2.9.1999 5:34 (Simon) ((no image)) Have you done anything in Hvitträsk besides taking pictures and recording sounds? Eh, there were some posters with textb. Simon

Notice how in Message 9.4, Kaisa describes Erik's behavior as "photo diarrhea," suggesting that he is sick. This description of course brings to mind foul odors and the less-than-pleasant necessity of cleaning up the mess. Here, the suggestion is that Erik is soiling the others' environment, forcing them to clean it up, just like parents have to clean up the mess when children have diarrhea.

In another case reported by Battarbee and Koskinen (2004), Thomas teases his babysitter Jani, who has suggested that Thomas could handle the toddler Mikey's evening tantrum by buying him a ball. However, Jani's well-meaning suggestion is used by Thomas as an opportunity to snap at Jani by comparing him to Mikey. By comparing Jani to a baby, he has pointed out that Jani is not to be taken seriously. Categories like these are not just a collection of sense-making means, but may also be ordered into a hierarchy. Putting someone into a "lower" category in a system in which he is entitled to a higher place is a useful insult. The correct choice after such a message is for the recipient to stop doing wrong and in this way reinstate his rights as a respectable and a serious person. Continuing with the behavior proves the new category to be correct and may prompt more tease (Sacks 1972a; Drew 1987; Kurvinen 2003).

Teasing in Closings

Message 9.6 provides an instance of closing with a tease, which is a particularly prevalent method of closing. Again, we meet Markku. A few days earlier, he had successfully reported on his trip to Vaasa, a West coast town, with a series of messages that had been welcomed by the recipients with compliments and questions. However, he continued to report his whereabouts when he returned to Helsinki, where he and most of his recipients live. In the first Helsinki message, taken from the Helsinki zoo, he sent a photograph of a tropical fish with his greetings. On the next day, he sent another tourist-like series with a photograph of a beach in one of Helsinki's more posh marinas, and then another photograph from a tourist boat. In both messages, he explained in detail where he was and what tourist attractions could be seen in the background.

While such messages may be interesting when they come from friends visiting other places, they were utterly boring for Markku's recipients, who all lived in the Helsinki region. Essentially, Markku was turning the

Message 9.6
Pauli to Markku

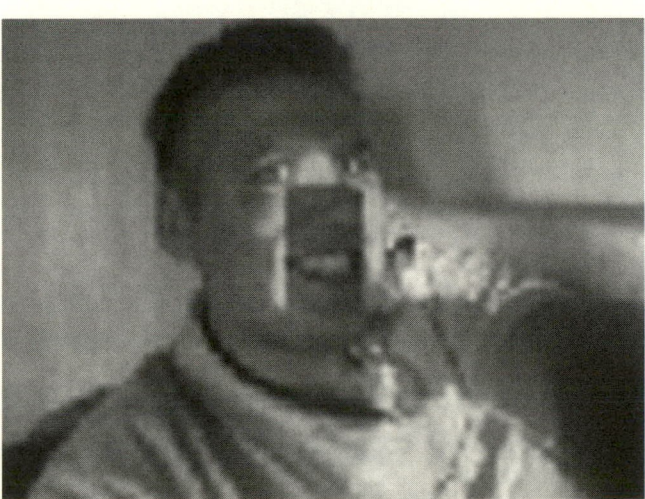

You're a helluva tourist...

best-known tourist attractions of his hometown into something special, even though for these people, they were ordinary places. What followed was a message in which Pauli teased Markku for being a "helluva tourist" with a photograph of his own, smiling face. This message characterizes Markku's activity as something improper and out-of-place, something fit for a tourist, but not for a local. With the tease, there is no need to explicitly ask Markku to stop sending these messages. Finally, there is the smile, which does two things: it shows that his tease is done in a friendly tone, and it may also show that there is something laughable in what Markku is doing.

This instance is a typical example of how a tease can be used in closing an exchange. Only twenty minutes later (17:06) Markku responds with still another photograph in which he says that he is indeed a tourist in Helsinki (he had moved to the city for his studies), and continues to tell how he is drinking cider with a young woman, who is in the background. However, he got the point and stopped sending boring tourist-like photographs.

Being Considerate in Closings by Doing Relational Work

Closing suggestions normally incorporate accounts and disclaimers that mitigate the impact of the closing. Typical examples of such accounts and disclaimers are humor, excuses, justifications, and hedges (Scott and Lyman 1968; Hewitt and Stokes 1975). With these devices, the communication channel is kept open despite the interactional problems posed by the closing.

Closings contain a great deal of what can be called relational work (Schegloff 1986) which helps people maintain their relationships regardless of these embarrassing actions (Goffman 1967). We have already seen that most closings are largely indirect: people employ teases and other indirect tactics to make sure their actions are not culpable. However, people are considerate in more complex ways, too. As an example, we can examine the following series, a continuation of the Markku series discussed above.

Markku had sent sightseeing photographs from Helsinki all day long, and Pauli had just called him a "tourist" (see Message 9.6). Message 9.7 is Markku's response to Pauli's tease. In this message, Markku jokefully ratifies this description, and adds that he is drinking cider. In so doing, he also sends a photograph of himself with a girl from a boat (as the flag in the background shows).

Leila got the message from Pauli, and noticed that Markku's photograph included a girl she does not know. In Message 9.8, she asks who she is, and also asks for a new photograph of her, "trading" a photograph of a man for this picture. Through this image, she reveals something of her life to others, which may be taken as a gift that must first be accepted and then reciprocated (Taylor and Harper 2002; Licoppe and Heurtin 2001). In Message 9.9, Markku sends the asked-for photograph, but also notes that he is suspicious of such "I trade you" deals, and does not reveal the girl's name. He also turns down the moral implicit in the notion of "I trade you" by labeling it a questionable practice.

Taken as a whole, Message 9.9 may be thought of as a rude response, which is evident in that Markku does many kinds of relational work in his message. First, there is a smiley (:-)), familiar to us from e-mail, the Web, and SMS messages (see Kasesniemi 2003: 203–207; Lorente et al. 2002). Second, there is a series of verbal gestures that mitigate his action. For example, when he says that he is sending the message "in response to the previous message," he shows that he would not have sent it without these preceding messages. Third, he places his suspicions about "I trade you's" in brackets instead of offering them in a weightier place. Finally, he ends his message with a question, which becomes the most prominent item for the recipient. Leila is not left with a rejection, but with a question indicating that Markku wants to keep on communicating.

Messages 9.7
Response to Pauli

Well I am a tourist in Helsinki... With cider.

Message 9.8
Identification Request Leila to Markku

I'll trade you this one for a picture of the girl!

Message 9.9
Identification from Markku to Leila

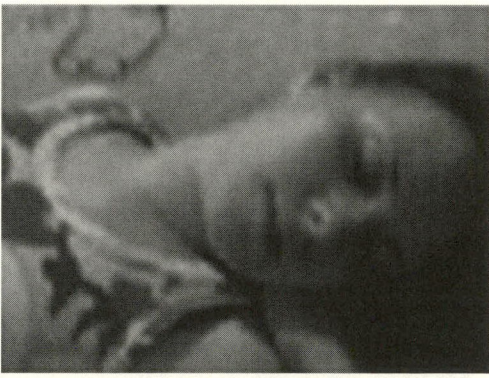

What was it that the professor was asking? In response to the previous message, here's the picture of the flower girl (even though I'm suspicious about such I trade you's...) Is the man in the picture Mr. Library? :)

With all this work, he makes an indirect apology for being rude, and provides a face-saver for Leila. Leila also gets a way out of his possible challenge: she can proceed to the new topic, Mr. Library. Later, Leila turned the discussion to Ms. Library instead of making Markku's reproach of the girl an issue. Thus, Markku was successful in his attempt to close messaging on the "flower girl," and turn messaging onto a new track without insulting Leila.

Mitigations like these are typical of closings. If we look at the previous messages in this Chapter, they all have their share of such mitigations. For example, Message 9.6 was a friendly tease, which leaves several face-saving options open for the recipient. Similarly, Message 9.2 has a greeting, and its possible tease is in the form a question, not a straightforward judgment, which leaves the final say to Erik. In turn, Message 9.3 has a ritualistic "thank you," and even though the message is an accusation and labels Erik "crazy," these items make the message so overblown that it comes to have a humorous, teasy overtone. Humor in particular plays a mitigating role in messages that drive messaging towards termination.

Reconciliations for Being Rude

Relational work is not always packed into one message: closings may take more than one message. Just as in talk, people often withdraw from interaction gradually over several turns especially if they have been talking about troubles (see Jefferson 1988).

The following example shows how such a process works. Again, we can continue to follow Markku, who did not stop with Message 9.9. Next, he sent Leila two photographs of his cats, and a photograph of flowers and plants at his home in a good night message even though no one demanded an apology or accused him of being rude. Pictures of cats function much like return gifts (Taylor and Harper 2002) aimed at reconciliation. In Message 9.10, a cat becomes a vehicle for taking attention away from the "flower girl." His chattiness in Message 9.11 further increases distance from the rejection. Finally, the plant message presents another gift, a photograph of flowers, continues with a chatty tone, adds a cliché towards the end, and finally has a good night wish, which is normally a proper reason to withdraw from interaction. (Message 9.12 was already analyzed as Message 8.7).

Message 9.10
Cat

Markku to Leila
Here's a picture of another beauty, for a while.

Message 9.11
Cat

Markku to Leila
And Tane is beautiful as well. A good picture. Tane got interested in a baby's cry outside. Perhaps he was in a family with children before.

**Message 9.12
Plants**

Markku to Leila
There are plants as well. It's really hot – I have to sleep on the floor. Kauko's playing; seek, boy, seek. Sometimes life is like dream. G'night.

As this example shows, by extending a closing over several messages, one can create a broad platform for many kinds of mitigating activities. By the end of Message 9.12, Markku has introduced almost a dozen reconciliatory items into his messages. The cat photographs work like gifts to settle Leila's mind. Furthermore, the last two messages direct attention to such trivialities as Tane the Cat's possible history, hot weather, and rock music ("Kauko" refers to a rock singer). Finally, the last message ends with two details that effectively close messaging. There is an idiom at the end of the message; idioms are typically used to close topics (Drew and Holt 1988). Also, there is a good night wish. With this gradual withdrawal, Markku has steered the exchange away from an unwanted topic, while simultaneously managing to make up for his earlier, and possibly rude, cut-off.

Of course, all this effort shows that for Markku, the fact that he almost turned down Leila's request to get the photograph of the girl was a tough call. However, as mentioned above, he was successful. This is typically so: there was only one instance of serious quarreling in both data sets. It took place, however, in a shaky relationship which was about to break up, not in normal chatty messaging.

Conclusions

Mobile multimedia can be analyzed as a sequence that begins when someone observes something interesting and reports it to others, who may respond. After a few messages, the exchange is typically over, and participants return to their previous activities. For a brief moment, however, they create and maintain a shared point of reference. It is this interactivity that makes mobile multimedia different from such traditional media forms as photographs and postcards. As we have seen, nighttime acts as a natural closing point and among couples at least, its significance is often specifically marked with good night messages aimed at closing messaging in a polite and affectionate manner.

As we have seen also, there are several reasons for closing. For example, regardless of measures used to secure the recipient's interest (analyzed in Chapter 7), banality may remain a problem in mobile multimedia. These devices follow people everywhere, opening everyday life for photographic reflection. Yet not everything can be made interesting. Some messages and items in them simply remain uninteresting enough not to elicit a response. Jokes get old. Other messages may be raunchy and plainly too sexist for the recipients. At worst, the message may embarrass the recipient and even threaten his reputation (see Gross and Stone 1964; Goffman 1967). Such messages may even lead to attempts to rebuke the sender and reprimand him in some fashion.

This reasoning leads to a question of methods used in closing messages. Perhaps the most prevalent feature of closings is that they are almost always indirect; in the massive data analyzed for this book, there was not a single instance of a direct closing in which the sender asked his interlocutors to stop sending messages in a verbal form. Still, closings are methodic. As examples of typical closing methods, this Chapter analyzed teases and status degradations, and demonstrated that people do lots of what I have called "being considerate" in conjunction with closings. Most closings take only one message, but the sender may spread it over a series of several messages. In all, people were remarkably successful in avoiding confrontations; in those few instances in which messaging escalated into something akin to quarrelling, the reasons typically went back to strained personal relationships.

Part IV

Society on the Phone

10

Society on the Small Screen

This Chapter focuses on how multimedia phones connect people to society. How is society built into messages? Does society remain mere backdrop, just something people can see in messages? Or does it also become something to be talked to? If it does, how do people make society a topic, and how do they maintain discussion on it?

This question is new in studies of mobile multimedia, which have focused almost exclusively on small groups. Existing research seems to reveal a sociable technology that has relatively little impact on society, and which is used mainly to document small issues in ordinary life—issues that scarcely have any bearing on the institutional structures of society. This is the basic message of studies in Italy (Scifo 2005), Japan (Okabe and Ito 2004), Finland (Koskinen 2007b), and France (Rivière 2005). Also, if anything, the previous chapters provide further evidence for this interpretation. The messages people design and share with others focus on the ordinary things of everyday life. They are designed to be meaningful for family, partners, friends, and acquaintances, and are circulated to people with whom one is already connected. Mobile multimedia thus appears to deepen existing ties rather than connect people to society. People come to elaborate their understanding of things in messages in these small circles.

This Chapter takes a fresh look at this conclusion by examining the most important ways in which society at large gets built into multimedia messages. How do institutions like politics, the economy, or religion appear in multimedia? In the following analysis, I have followed two principles (see Schegloff 1992). First, society has to be made relevant in messages somehow, for example through references to social groups or categories. If there are no such references, then the issue is not relevant in interaction. Secondly, these references have to have at least some bearing on action. If they do not have consequences for action, they simply remain background elements. Thus, if one takes a photograph of a baby running in front of the Parliament, a key social institution no doubt appears in the photograph. However, if it is not specifically made into a political object by, say, admiring the home of democracy, it remains just a scenic element rather than shows orientation to political, social, economic, or religious issues.

Media as a Source of Social Commentary

Society becomes a topic in mobile multimedia mainly through the media. People do not just render society visible in messages through media quotes, but they may also take sides on what they see and read. The media surrounds us with rich, visual, professionally created imagery from which people can pick up not just images, but also ideas, and formats for constructing new ways of using the camera. People capture items from many types of media, including all kinds of screens, print sources, posters and postcards and various types of product graphics.

Politics and economics are important for modern media, which follows these aspects of society closely. What happens to media coverage of political, economic, and religious affairs in multimedia messages? Do these institutions appear at all in the small space provided by a message? As Katz (2005) has shown, at least religion constantly appears in phones, as people do take photographs of priests, ministers, religions symbols, as well as churches. Why not political and economic institutions? As such, many participants in the study were well prepared to make observations about society because of their education and studies.

Usually media appeares in an ambient role only, as in Message 10.1, in which Petri asks for a piece of practical information from Annemari with a picture of President Bush giving a speech. The picture has some value in communication, as it suggests that Petri is watching television. However, it has no relationship whatsoever to the very action noted in the message.

Curiously, if we go beyond such ambient uses, references to the economy and politics were virtually nonexistent in media quotes. The economy in particular became relevant mainly through sarcastic comments on the prices of goods. In one case, Ari took a photograph of a headline in a tabloid, which accused the head of Nokia's multimedia unit of pricing the first multimedia phones too high. Sarcastically, Ari agreed in text by writing, "795 [Euros] is a pretty high price, got to say." However, this message hardly displays signs of economic thinking or political

Message 10.1
((No subject))

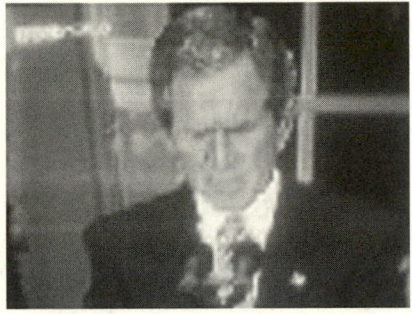

Petri_to_Annemari
Ask Leila when she gets out so that I can prepare food for her.

Message 10.2
Markku to Leila

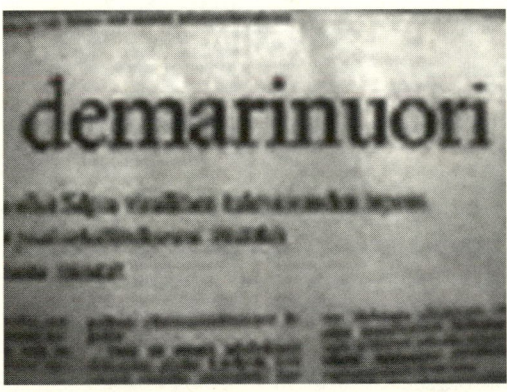

THE VISIBLE WORD IN PHOTOGRAPH: "Young Social Democrat"
TEXT WRITTEN BY MARKKU: Hah! Bourgeois you say... Never!

consciousness. Rather, it corroborates the conclusion that multimedia is tightly rooted in everyday life rather than in institutional life.

It was equally difficult to find politics in messages. As we have seen, even when politicians like George Bush appeared in photographs, they appeared in ambient roles only. Politicians became eye-candy, and their photographs showed what the sender was doing (watching TV) at the time that he was designing the message.

Message 10.2 is one of the few examples in which people expressed their political opinions in multimedia. Reading Markku's message, Leila had apparently teased him about his "bourgeois" opinions. Markku takes this as a well-meaning insult, and responds with a long, jocular message, of which I will only show the first part. In no uncertain terms, he denies having bourgeois sympathies, and adds a photograph that tells where his political sympathies lie. This is politics that is a far cry from heated debate in the town hall, which epitomizes direct democracy.

As noted in the introductory Chapter, there are two studies that make the claim that text messages and mobile phones may affect the course of political events in important ways. First, Dányi and Sükösd (2003) demonstrate how text messages were used in the 2002 Hungarian parliamentary elections to mobilize the electorate to attend demonstrations and public meetings, for political marketing, and for spreading politically motivated humor. Secondly, in the Philippines, President Joseph Estrada reputedly fell victim to the power of SMS (send text messages) in 2001 (Rheingold 2003a: 157–160). Against expectations, there is no evidence to support this thesis in *Mobile Image* and *Radiolinja*. After all, it is easy to imagine people exchanging messages in which they take photographs of misleading advertisements, and send them to consumer groups or authorities. In our studies, however, part of the reason for political inaction may have been the time of year: during the summer vacation season, the media does not focus much on politics, but is rather more likely to follow entertainment than more serious issues. During the study period, no significant economic or political events on the scale of the fall of the Berlin Wall took place.

Entertainment as Institution: Stalking Celebrities

People encounter things important to society not only in media, but also in their lives. Do they capture things they see and share them, showing social awareness that way? What kinds of things do they capture?

The most common institution that enters mobile multimedia messaging is no doubt entertainment through celebrity culture. For example, in

Mobile Image, taking pictures of celebrities started immediately. The set of celebrities who got into mobile phones consisted of the usual suspects: actors, rock stars, musicians, TV personalities, beauty queens, and politicians. Message 10.3 is the first message sent in the female group in *Mobile Image*. One of the members, Kathy, had spotted a celebrity violin player on the street, and tried to take a photograph of her, with little success. This sort of celebrity spotting took place in all of the groups studied. Of course, we do not know how many celebrities went without being photographed, but it was standard practice to capture and report seeing famous people when they were spotted.

The practice took several more complex forms, as in one case in which the camera was too slow to get a photograph of a former Miss Finland,

Message 10.3
Kathy testing…

I thought to start picture messaging with a picture of Linda Brando, but I was too slow. You can only see Linda as a set of white hair next to the traffic sign. The camera is nice. Ken will soon take the phone down the tubes because all I do these days is that I gossip to the phone and read e—mail… I'm not sure about what happens if I send an image to people outside the research group. Does it end up to data?Have a nice day, Kathy

who was seen in the Casino in Hanko, a southern tourist destination and harbor town. In a message to her friends Anne writes about this incident: "Miss Finland Suvi Miinala sitting on the front stairs of the Hanko Casino when we walked by." However, she continues: "(Peter recognized her, I didn't). Since we didn't get a picture of her, we took a picture of her picture" (Tue, 20 Jun 2000 0:19).

This message has two interesting features. The first is obvious: if the camera is too slow, or the cameraman too shy, it is always possible to find pictures of entertainers in tabloids and gossip weeklies. The second one is more interesting. There is a degree of discreetness in this behavior. People exhibited in several ways that they knew that celebrities are supposed to have a right to privacy, and taking photographs of them is either banal, or intrusive enough to be avoided. Thus, in celebrity photographs, there is usually a degree of self-parody and self-depreciation. In the Hanko Casino message, Anna keeps her distance from celebrity culture by making it clear that it was not she who recognized Miss Finland, but her male companion.

Both data sets demonstrate that mobile multimedia in ordinary people's hands does produce a continuous stream of photographs of celebrities (see also Ito 2004). However, such practice of taking pictures of celebrities can hardly be called "stalking," which suggests a conscious, spy-like activity rather than what we see in these data. People do take photographs of people in the public eye when they see them, but this behavior is not like *paparazzi* journalism, which in its tough forms borders on harassment. Rather, a good deal of celebrity photographing can be called accidental celebrity-spotting rather than stalking. Yet there may be seeds of civil action here. Politicians and captains of industry are often celebrities. If people routinely pay attention to them when they spot them in public, and use multimedia phones to capture footage from them, under certain circumstances this footage may become a means of political action. Amateur footage of an intoxicated presidential candidate in a bar might change the course of the nation for years to come.

Ideology in Action

The above observations inevitably lead to the conclusion that mobile multimedia is not a particularly political vehicle. However, this is not the case when we situate this technology in social organization. To state this in the simplest possible way: people who are accustomed to seeing things in political terms and to demonstrate use mobile multimedia politically. Less politically active people end up taking other types of images that contribute to other types of social structures in which macro-level social issues may not play a particularly important role. People who lead politically active lives observe things using methods reflective of their ideologies and theories about society, and use these same methods in reporting their observations. When people view issues politically, they come to introduce politics into the new technological domain, making it a relevant item for action that follows.

To show how such a process takes place, let us turn to the female group of *Mobile Image*, which consisted of sociology students. This group did develop something akin to a political multimedia culture. Their texts in particular are full of "sociologuese," which can be defined as a semi-academic vernacular suitable for making big-picture observations about social issues like poverty and power.

There are no examples of openly political messages in this group, but we may find instances of sociologuese in many details of messages. In Message 10.4, two young women pose for the camera on a balcony and call themselves "suburban mothers" in a clearly disparaging tone. The message is a friendly tease to the boyfriend of one of the women, and the "suburban issue" is clearly a side issue. However, disdain of suburbs in this message is typical to an urban educated middle class on aesthetic, social and ecological grounds. Of course, the message is self-ironic, but it also displays an elaborate sociological attitude towards the suburban lifestyle.

Also, there was a hint of technological criticism in the messages of this group. They made several observations about how the ability to exchange visual messages changed their mutual relationships. In Message 10.5, two women are playing with their phones (the communicator) in a dark room. The text describes how technology is changing female friendships, transforming them into something "lighter than light."

While the tone of the message, in the best sociological tradition, is neutral, the writer can be seen to be giving priority to face-to-face communication over mediated communication. The notion of "lighter than light" forms of community probably comes from the French philosopher and sociologist Paul Virilio, who had at that time gained a following among sociologists at the University of Helsinki. Without going into Virilio's theories, the example well illustrates how sociology students go about seeing their world with sociological concepts.

In all, this group could hardly be more different from the male group in *Mobile Image*. As mentioned earlier, the male group developed a habit of portraying the opposite sex as an object of evaluation and desire

Message 10.4
Subject: Shock Treatment

Darling John,Here's real shock treatment for you, that is pictures from last summer night from our balcony with Minna and Mia. We took pictures from the future of suburban moms, that is, about how horrible we are not hopefully going to look like. But we do look horrible! I decided to give a shock treatment to your love! I'll write more later, now Sanna's waiting for us to the table.Best, Sue

Message 10.5
Subject: ((no subject))

Some things stay, some change. At the end of the Boulevard is a shipyard in which they build huge ships for the Caribbean, but what is changing is the friendship between girls. What else should you think about an evening a few days ago, when we tried to warm up the ice—cold Champaign, and while waiting, each party member went to write things with their Communicator. A new social form, even lighter than light community?

as a central theme of their sociability (Koskinen et al. 2002: ch. 7). In quantitative terms, less than half of the mobile visual messages were "girl pictures," in which women were displayed as objects of conquest. A comparison between these cultures shows how people who use different ethnomethods observe and report different things. While one sees sexual opportunities, another sees global issues at work. If we were to study politicians or consumer activists, we would surely find even more differences. Thus, there is no need to think that "the social" in mobile multimedia means having fun only with friends. Issues of great social importance may, and inevitably will, become "messaged" when these devices come to be used by people who, like the women in *Mobile Image*, have a social conscience. Mobile multimedia adds a new channel for social consciousness for people who care about society and want to change it.

Discussion and Conclusions

This Chapter has questioned one possible interpretation of mobile multimedia, namely, that it is primarily a technology that adds affective and social content to communication among people who are already closely linked (Scifo 2005; Koskinen 2007a; Rivière 2005). On the other hand, if social issues become topics in messaging, mobile multimedia may change society—perhaps a little like mobile phones have transformed the streets of Manila (Rheingold 2003a; Pertierra et al. 2002) and Hungarian elections (Dányi and Sükösd 2003).

This Chapter has shown that, in principle at least, people make society relevant in multimedia messaging just as easily as in conversation. As such, there is no radical difference between sending messages about politics, economy, religion, or the baby's activities. All it takes to make mobile multimedia a political tool is to capture a photograph of the drug addict on the street and turn that into a social commentary in text (or audio), explaining how the presence of junkies is evidence of social ills and the government's inability to deal with the problem. However, with the partial exception of the female group in *Mobile Image*, this did not happen. Most messaging focused on what we, following Gergen (2007), can call "immediate" life. People targeted their friends, pets, and other issues familiar to us from the Kodak culture (Chalfen 1987) rather than the political press or social documentary. Also, messages with references to, say, politics usually remained individual observations; they were not responded to. Society's significant institutions were not a matter of exchange in *Mobile Image* and *Radiolinja*.

Thus, with the qualifications given above, our data strengthen rather than question the conclusion that multimedia focuses on things of limited importance to society. When social structures appear in messages, they appear mainly as passing remarks or ambient items in mass media. As such, this orientation is not surprising. For most people in post-industrialized societies, political and social issues are matters discussed in the media rather than matters demanding personal involvement. Still, the limited means provided by the mobile phone appear to simplify political and social concerns into simple snapshots and personal, often sarcastic comments. Also, there is no evidence of anything like "town hall meetings" in phones. The difference to text messaging is important; text messaging has already proved to be an important instrument not only in the Philippines and Hungary, but also in coordinating demonstrations against the World Trade Organization, World Bank, or European Union in such places as Seattle and Gothenburg.

11

Friends and Acquaintances

The previous Chapter showed that multimedia messages tend to focus on everyday life rather than the more significant institutions of society. Even when society at large is targeted in messages, it remains a matter of fleeting commentary among friends and acquaintances. This Chapter takes this conjecture one step further by focusing on what mobile multimedia technology does in these monadic clusters by updating social information among friends and acquaintances.

The first two sections take a closer look at how people expand groups through introductions and identifications. Multimedia messaging offers two resources for these activities: with photographs and sound files, people can send visual and audio samples of previously unknown people to recipients. This feature makes it possible for them to maintain awareness of the social environment far better than with verbal descriptions in text messages or talk. In brief, the first two sections demonstrate that with mobile multimedia, people almost unwittingly construe, share, and maintain social maps of friends and acquaintances.

The third section turns to how messages update social information among friends and acquaintances. It is based on the observation that when people hear or see an activity, they may tie these activities to categories of people (for instance, "a sportsman"). Once such a category is formulated, people may attribute other activities and attitudes, rights and obligations, and social relations to these people (see Hester and Eglin 1997: 8–9). As we shall see, through visual and aural means, mobile multimedia deepens the way in which friends understand each other, partly through such categorization processes, partly by expanding their stock of knowledge.

The relevance of mobile multimedia in this context is that it conveys a wider array of life for inspection than, say, text messages in which the content is almost totally controllable by the sender. In multimedia, people come to deliver bits and pieces of their lives not just intentionally, but also in the background of the message and in its composition. With these bits and pieces, the recipients may alter their understanding of the sender. For example, if the recipients learn through a band picture that the sender, an accountant by trade, hangs out with heavy rock musicians, they may have to radically revise their opinions of the sender. Thus, although introductions, identifications and membership categories may appear mundane at first sight, these activities add significantly to the stock of social knowledge.

Persons in Messages: Introductions and Identifications

People routinely introduce people to their friends and acquaintances with their multimedia phones. Photographs in particular are useful in this respect. Typically, details of these identification messages show these people have been talked about previously. There are two main types of these messages: "Introductions" are initiated by a sender; "Identifications" start when a recipient asks about persons unknown to him or her.

The following two messages provide a simple case of introducing one's friends. In them, Leila introduces two people to Maria. In Message 11.1, she introduces Anu's husband to her. Message 11.2 introduces Anu. Several details of these messages show that Leila and Maria have been talking—or texting—previously about Anu. For example, Leila uses Anu's first name without adding any further details about her, thus showing that Leila thinks that Maria does not need more detail to know who she is hanging out with (Sacks and Schegloff 1979). Anu had never been mentioned in the *Radiolinja* data previously. The familiar tone, then, is grounded in gossip rather than in Maria's specific wish to learn to know Anu.

Message 11.1 has a further interesting detail. The picture shows that Anu's husband plays an instrument (guitar). From the text, the recipient can infer that Anu's husband is a jazz musician. The text highlights an element (a man in the image), but a crucial piece of information comes from the image, which becomes an active element in the message. As viewers, we learn not only the names of the people, but also can use the surroundings to communicate things in ways that would be far more difficult to communicate in text messages.

Identifications, the second person-oriented main practice in mobile multimedia, are recipient-initiated. When a recipient gets a message in which there are persons she does not know, she may ask about identification. For example, Message 11.3 shows three women, who are going out

Message 11.1
Introducing Anu

Leila to Maria
Jazz is playing hard, and it is really nice out here. The character on the left is Anu's husband.

Message 11.2
Introducing Anu

Leila to Maria
And here's Anu.

for the evening. One of them is unknown to Markku, who asks who she is in Message 11.4. In Message 11.5, Mari replies to him the next morning. She also describes her hangover and plans for the next evening. In conversational analytic terms, Messages 11.4 and 11.5 make an adjacency pair: not replying to Message 11.3 would have been noticeable (Schegloff and Sacks 1973; Sacks 1995, II: 521–532). With them, Markku achieves what he was up to: getting to know who Mari was out with.

Thus, introductions and identifications may come to carry meaningful social information. In interviews, members of the women's group in *Mobile Image* described the significance of the social information they shot and shared with their devices:

> For her part, Mervi says that she has only seen Liisa's new boyfriend in digital pictures. Similarly, Eija had sent and shown pictures not only to her group and her boyfriend, but also to her friends and relatives: "My mother saw a picture of my boyfriend for the first time on the screen of the digital camera." Introducing family, partners and friends was similar in both the young women's and the young men's group. (Koskinen et al. 2002: 85)

In this context, photographs perform important work. They give recipients a possibility for inferences that would not be possible with just talk or text. Leila manages to show that Anu's husband is a jazz musician without saying anything about his occupation. Markku was only able to

Message 11.3
An Evening Out

Mari to Markku
We always have fun!

Message 11.4
Who is Marie?

Markku to Mari
Wow! One of the best pictures of you. You look really good, I must admit. Who is Marie? And who's the fourth one? Emma?

Message 11.5
Who is Marie?

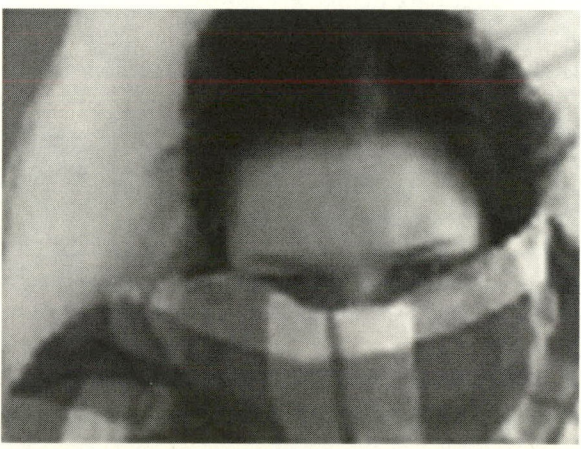

Mari to Markku
What a redneck! AnnMARIA of course… In the middle in the group picture is Emma, and on the left Emma's friend whose name escapes me. I'm feeling bad, sweaty, and feel like throwing up, and I must go to work today. Then I have to buy a swimsuit, and as a bonus, train ride to Jyväskylä to Betonirock. Oh my God :)

be curious about the fourth woman because there was an image. Markku's message furthermore shows how such inferences become available for viewers, and how they can be installed in interaction as queries that lead to improved shared understanding.

Case Study: Introductions and Identifications in *Mobile Image*

To see how introductions and identifications work over time, we may look at Kata, a young woman who participated in the second group of *Mobile Image*. She was picked randomly from all participants in the two studies reported in this book. During the two months of the study, she introduced seventeen people to her friends in her messages. Four of these were her family, but she also introduced her boyfriend both to other women in the group and to acquaintances in Europe (in her case, Spain and France). Other people who appeared in her messages were acquaintances; two were children. It is noticeable that most of them were introduced in images: only one of them, a well-known young artist, appeared in text only. Also, she conscientiously explained in text who appeared in images. The only exception to this rule was a sauna picture from a Midsummer party, in which six unidentified people were cooling off on a balcony outside the sauna.

To see how her messages work, we may look in detail at two messages she sent to other members of the women's group (Messages 11.6 and 11.7). She was visiting her relatives outside Helsinki, and also met her parents and sister. On their way back from the town of Tampere, they made a "nostalgic trip" to their earlier homes in suburban Helsinki. In Kata's two messages, she not only introduced her family, but also revealed several previously unknown details of her life to her friends. Hyvinkää and "Kervo City" are small towns in the vicinity of Helsinki, the latter a suburb, the former a town north of the greater metropolitan area.

In these two messages, Kate sends seven pictures in which she introduces her family. In addition, she provides a host of contextual cues for making sense of these messages. First, people in pictures get "roles" in her family. Secondly, the signature "the suburban child" in the first message shows that she is neither from Helsinki proper, nor from a small town or the countryside.

These pictures do more work than just introduce her family. For example, she shows her homes. In essence, they are typical middle-class homes. However, they are placed in a series that describes her family history. Early in her life, the family was living in a flat, but moved to

Messages 11.6
Nostalgy, Part I

The Koivu family reunion: for the first time for years, Kata, Mary, mom and dad in Tampere with relations. On our way back to the Karjala of a postmodern child, first to Hyvinkää to see the hospital in which Kata was born, and then the first home of the reconstituted family of Koivu, which was also Kata's home for the first 5 months. Here are pictures from the home and art on its yard. br. the suburban child

**Message 11.7
Part II**

The Hyvinkää hospital and two former homes from Kervo City. Kata
((3 pictures omitted))

a more expensive form of housing over the years. The second message shows a townhouse with its own yard, and a one-family house with a long driveway and a large yard. The series shows that the family fortunes have been getting consistently better over the years, although the starting point was not glorious.

This case study shows that at best, mobile multimedia may become an important social glue. Kata introduced roughly two new people to others every week, increasing their understanding of her social life and network remarkably. As a result, they learned to know her background, her hobbies, and her family life.

Hobbies and Activities as a Basis for Categorization

Mobile multimedia updates and deepens social knowledge between close friends for a simple reason. Often information about friends remains unknown to people, even though it might be relevant to understanding. People categorize each other using their knowledge of them: if they know someone is "sporty" or "likes to travel," they mold their plans and expectations to fit this category (Hester and Eglin 1997). If they learn that someone cheats at card games, they may change their behavior towards that person (Hannerz 1967). With new bits and pieces of information, people categorize and sometimes re-categorize their friends, giving new angles to their relationship.

As Kata's case illustrates, mobile multimedia comes in handy in such work. With it, people are able not only to introduce new people to recipients, but also to present new information about themselves. Typically, this information is about activities of which others are well aware. If one goes to jazz concerts or rock festivals, and sends several pictures from these occasions, others learn about one's taste in music.

First of all, categorizations take place constantly in day-to-day activities. To give an example, there is an instance in *Radiolinja* in which Ari, a young man, reports his activities during the first day of his holiday. In the first message, sent at 07:43, he tells that his holiday has just started, and adds a cheerful yell to describe his mood. During the next few hours, he sends several more messages. At 08:37 he wonders why no one is sending any messages to him with a picture of his buttocks. At 09:47, he sends a picture of an ostrich, texting that it is his friend and adding a voice sample in which he mimics duck, hen, and pig. Finally, at 12:12 he sends a picture of his face and upper torso. He is waving his finger, asking "what the fuck" is happening while peppering this text with a loud shout "GR:::::::A::::::,h:::" in audio. All these messages were sent to the whole group, that is, ten people, who get evidence of what he is doing. Through these messages, he comes to show how he is spending the first day of his holiday.

After receiving the messages described above, Anna, one of the recipients, sent Ari her best wishes for a good holiday. She also formulated her inference about what he is going to do while vacationing with a picture of a cocktail glass (this graphic was available in her phone) and an audio file saying: ".hhh Have a wi/ld r:\ide Ari (0.3) /Ciao \ciao". The expression "wild ride" is key here: in local parlance, it is a euphemism for binge drinking. For Anna, Ari had given enough evidence of his holiday plans to warrant such an inference. Other responses to his message follow a similar pattern. At 10:55, Sam sent a picture from a street bar, saying that "it tastes good at the street bar," and at 21:07, Tom sent a picture of an empty beer glass with no text or sound. Through these messages, Anna, Sam, and Tom showed that they understood perfectly well that Ari was drinking.

Sometimes even close friends engage in activities unfamiliar to each other. In viewing and listening to multimedia messages, one may become aware of these activities, which then color one's understanding of the sender. For example, if one does like Kata, and repeatedly visits flea markets selling goods manufactured by the native populations of South America, and installs Spanish words into her messages, showing familiarity with South American cultures, such knowledge will come to color the recipients' understanding of her. Another example is Jari, who had a habit of documenting his activities conscientiously to his friends. Perhaps the most dramatic example is in Message 11.8, which he sent in March after the skydiving season had just opened.

Through messages like this one, Jari's friends got a far better understanding of him. Although in interviews, the participants said that the pictures did not reveal essentially new features about their friends' personalities, they also said that messages introduced them better to each others' acquaintances. For example, Tapani said that he "got a glimpse of where they had been, all those things which used to be in the dark," and Tommy said in the interview that he was even a little surprised when he saw how varied Jari's leisure time activities were. In his turn, Jari responded that it was fun to be able to visually tell about his activities:

> These are just the things I am always talking about, and this is that gang and this is what we are up to and here is our boat.... This mobile visual message group has now become aware of many of the other social circles I have been part of, like there were

some of those parachuting pictures. No one in that group had seen before what kind of a gang it is and what kinds of parties they have and what that activity is all about. (Koskinen et al. 2002: 85)

An important observation appears in the beginning of the quote. Although mobile multimedia messages create mutual awareness between close friends, they may not change the perception of personalities. It is hardly surprising that people who have known each other for a long time do not change their understanding of each other as persons. They have been exposed to each other several times in a variety of circumstances in which they have construed an understanding of others' tempers, habits, and attitudes, among other things. If we believe the men in *Mobile Image*, multimedia messages do not significantly change such core conceptions of others. However, they still bring knowledge that leads to subtler changes in mutual understanding.

Message 11.8
Season Opening

Subject: Skydive
hi guysseason opening!!!180 km/h and —20°C
JK

Conclusions

This Chapter has analyzed two ways in which mobile multimedia functions in small groups of people by adding social knowledge. Senders' introductions and recipients' identification requests both lead to an increase in social knowledge, and a better mutual understanding of multimedia partners' social circles. To an extent, they work as the "Jewish geography," a social game in which people identify and locate people in terms of social networks and social status and, sometimes, establish mutual acquaintances (Yerkovich 1976: 36).

We have also seen that when people see activities and relationships in messages, they may formulate what they see in terms of membership categories and thus generalize from what they see to more permanent traits. People do make inferences about each other using visual and audio elements in multimedia messages; what counts as "information" are not just activities, but also issues such as opinions and attitudes evident in messages. Once such categorization has been made, people may use that to deduce what kinds of activities, opinions, and preferences others have (see Sacks 1972a, 1972b; Hester and Eglin 1997; Jayysi 1984).

It is relatively easy to show that introductions, identifications, and membership categorical descriptions bear on action on a local basis. For example, membership categorizations in teases are ordinarily devised to close messaging that has gone too far (see Chapter 9). Of course, even these inferences renew and shape communities and groups. However, at present, we lack the data to study possible longer-lasting functions of categorizations and re-categorizations. Thus, the question of whether mobile multimedia changes the ways in which social action beyond the local context is shaped remains open. In any case, the analysis presented in this and the previous Chapter provides further support to the idea that mobile multimedia is primarily a technology that people use in monadic clusters (Gergen 2006).

12

From Small Discoveries to Stable Activities

This Chapter elaborates and generalizes the picture of the two previous chapters, but poses a new question. Previously, we have seen how people capture and share things in society using traditional, culturally established categories and formats. However, this Chapter shows that they are not bound by these categories: they also develop new categories in interaction with others. Is mobile multimedia a creative instrument? And if so, how do people come to develop new versions of methods they originally used in designing messages?

The observation that people use electronic devices in ways that differ from the "scripts" engineers have designed into them is not new. For example, when the Walkman broke through to the mass market, it was widely condemned for increasing isolation in society. With earphones on, people would not be alert to each other in public places; instead, they would only concentrate on their own affairs and pleasures. Scholars soon argued against this vision, maintaining instead that when people use the Walkman, they can in fact impose their own experience and order over situations that are otherwise out of their control (Hosokawa 1984; Bull 2000). Others soon pointed out that using a mass-produced device to do what it was designed for in the first place can hardly be taken as a creative act (du Gay et al. 1997).

These arguments have resurfaced with digital technology and mobile telephony. Some evidence shows that people use these technologies creatively, appropriating them into their lives, always molding them for their own purposes. Sometimes, these purposes are not those that appeared on the designers' drawing boards. The best-known example is no doubt text messaging, which rose from obscurity to become a world-changing technology (Kasesniemi 2003; Lorente et al. 2002). Similarly, with mobile phones, people can appropriate the city, turning into comfortable living rooms places that were previously meaningless and boring (Kopomaa

2000). This argument has several precursors in literature on the Internet and the Web (Murray 1999; Negroponte 1999).

However, several studies have argued otherwise, that technology is not necessarily used creatively. For example, in their ethnography of the Internet in Trinidad, Miller and Slater (2000) noted that personal communication on the Internet—like teasing and gossip (*commess*)—is concentrated in discussion groups, chat and IRC, while www. sites proper follow more traditional models of advertising and publishing activities. On commercial www. sites, images and graphics are usually made by professionals. The argument that people author content in the digital domain using age-old practices, of course, was voiced by Taylor and Harper (2002) in their study on text messaging. This was also the main thrust of *Mobile Image* (Koskinen et al. 2002), which showed how people borrow methods for constructing and replying to messages from ordinary life.

Ultimately, this Chapter raises an old question about users' creativity, but respecifies it. Thus far, this book has shown that people build their multimedia messages on practices inherited from snapshot photography, media genres, and on many kinds of age-old practices like asking and answering questions. However, there is also evidence of more creative uses, as shown by stories like *Murder at Lammassaari* (Message 4.5) and the analysis of responses in Chapter 8. This Chapter examines the issue of creative usage by analyzing how people invent these methods while doing things with other people. The aim is to show that creative acts are taking place constantly, but only a few develop into permanent resources of action. This Chapter focuses on how these small discoveries happen and become stable features not only of individual action but also of social action.

Discovering Image Manipulation in *Mobile Image*

The question posed in this Chapter has its origins in an observation made during *Mobile Image*. The activities of the pilot group in that study took an unexpected track when two members started to manipulate images with image processing software before sending them. That is, they downloaded images from mobile devices to their computers, manipulated them, and sent them back after changes. They utilized one "affordance" of the digital domain: the possibility to manipulate images digitally.

This discovery came about slowly. Although the pilot group began to download images from the Web fairly early in the pilot—first image taken from the Web was a picture of an I-Mac on June 30, 1999—the first image manipulation was sent only about a month later, on July 27. This picture, sent by Simon, showed two members of the group, but the background was changed into a colorful, incomprehensible maze. A week later, Erik sent a photograph of a statue located in Central Helsinki wearing a mobile phone. Three days later, he sent technical information about server connections using his self-portrait instead of a signature. Two hours and 13 minutes later, Simon responded to him with a manipulated image embedded in a tease. In his message, Erik was wearing a suit instead of a t-shirt. Simon had also added the national flag to the background. In text, he transformed the "server" into "serving his country," and Erik was identified as the former president of the country. In Simon's response, the original message was set into a new gestalt contexture (Gurwitsch 1964) that changed its meaning entirely. This example was analyzed in Messages 8.12–8.13.

While the first modification of the gestalt contexture had turned a co-worker into a former president, the next few messages generalized this new contexture, and established image manipulation as a new *modus operandi* for the group. The next day, Simon sent his own visual self-

Message 12.1
"Two Designers"

Hi,So, me and Kaisa have digitized our pictures into the address book of the commie

portrait, but used the actor Liam Neeson's face instead of his own. The message also had greetings from Kaisa, another member of the pilot group, but instead of her face, Simon used that of the actress Gillian Anderson (see Koskinen et al. 2002: 72–73).

The discovery that it is relatively easy to manipulate images and make communication more fun that way soon led to other discoveries. Since *Star Wars I: The Phantom Menace* was running in movie theaters at the time, it was easy to find pictures of Liam Neeson in practically every corner of the city. Four days later, Ilkka sent a photograph of a Pizza Hut poster with Liam Neeson dressed as a character from the movie. In text, he wondered why on earth Simon is advertising fast food in a weird uniform. Erik picked up the joke: when he was watching the movie *Rob Roy* starring Liam Neeson on television, he photographed Neeson from the television and sent the photograph the next day with the heading "Simon the Furious." (See Koskinen et al. 2002: 73–74).

After seeing this message, other members of the group discovered that with digital manipulations, friends could be made to play parts in imaginary worlds. This was a typical small discovery, which, of course, is not unique to the digital realm. For instance, popular culture and everyday life typically intertwine in children's games, in sports, and in the minds of movie enthusiasts. Still, it shows how mobile multimedia provides tools for mixtures of reality and fantasy, and how individual creative acts become more stable resources of social action.

Riddles: Discovering and Elaborating Activities

When people first got multimedia phones in their hands and started to explore their expressive potentials, they largely relied on Taylor and Harper's (2002) age-old practices like greetings and questions. However, small discoveries take place even when people design their messages with such age-old practices. This section analyzes how one group developed a lively riddle culture during the first four days of the study, where about seventy messages were riddles. The interesting point is that these riddles were *always* based on images. In fact, every part of a riddle could be visual, not just the original puzzle (see Koskinen and Kurvinen 2005).

The first riddles followed the traditional three-part format analyzed in Chapter 8 (Messages 8.4-8.6). In this format, the riddle is followed by a guess by the recipient. If the guess is correct, it is acknowledged in the third message; if it is wrong, the third message provides the correct answer. Within a week, the structure of riddles became increasingly more varied, as people also learned to use at least the following:

- *Clues.* As already noted above, the sender may also provide clues to recipients.
- *Rewards.* When starting the riddle, a bonus of some kind can be offered. For example in one message a bottle of beer was promised to whomever was able to give the right answer.
- *Side sequences.* Other things that make this structure more complex are side sequences in which the recipient may, for example, ask for a reward if the guess proves to be right. Such inquiries are typically responded to either by promising a reward or by denying it.
- *Closing suggestions.* Recipients may show the sender that the riddle is getting boring by asking the joker to send the correct answer and by making disapproving remarks or gestures about the quality of the riddle.
- *Visual responses.* Recipients' remarks may be visual and lead to visual commentary that takes place aside from the actual textual exchange.

To take an example of some of these techniques at work, let us take a closer look at one riddle from the end of the first week of the study. At this stage, riddles routinely had several of these component parts. To begin with, the senders had learned to design increasingly more difficult riddles. For example, in one case, Anders sent a message of a fuzzy, dim mixture of red and blue light and asked others to guess what it was. He also promised two prizes, a cigarette and a bottle of beer, to those who guessed right, and made a less adult provision for Olli, a teenager, promising soda for him.

This message elicited a series of six messages. The first guess came from Mikko four minutes later. His guess was "the glove box of your car. Is that right?" Six minutes after Mikko, Ann-Marie guessed TV in a message without a photograph. Eleven minutes after her, it was Tom's turn to guess television, with a photograph of a TV set. Slightly later, Ann-Marie got bored, and requested the right answer with "What was it?" In response to Ann-Marie's request, Anders sent the right answer to everyone in the original list: in the photograph was his car stereo. However, Anders also described the riddle as "easy," and said that no prizes would be given because no one had gotten it right. He also added a photograph of his empty hand. Three minutes later, however, Mikko protested that his guess—the car—was partly right, and that he was therefore entitled to part of the prize, the cigarette. He added a photograph of a cactus, perhaps suggesting that the riddle was spiky, that is, too difficult.

As this example demonstrates, riddles may have a complex social organization. Typically, there is the joker, who initiates the sequence by posing the riddle, and closes it by providing the correct answer. Others participate in the riddle typically by guessing but, as mentioned above, they may also try to renegotiate rewards and try to close an episode that is getting too extensive. Not every riddle was sent to all participants. For instance, Anne received only one riddle on the first day, and did not respond, after which she was dropped from the list of recipients. Typically, even when the riddle was sent to several people, guesses were only sent to the joker, creating a momentary imbalance in the activity. However, in a couple of cases, guesses were shared with others, turning guesswork into a collective activity.

Perhaps the most interesting feature of riddles was that the other groups did not create a riddle culture, even though there were riddles in each group in *Mobile Image* and *Radiolinja*. Even in the group in focus, it was something of a fad. The first riddles were sent on the second day of the study, and the most prolific day was the fourth day, during which thirty-two messages were sent in four riddles. After four days, the number of riddles decreased significantly. The next two riddles were sent a week later, and the last ones a week after that. The last two weeks of the five-week period did not include any riddles. Such a pattern suggests that people pick up specific methods of action from others and use them with little reflection. When no one uses this particular method, it drops off the collective list of stable methods.

Discovering Sound

People not only discover methods of action, but also technical possibilities in their devices. How people discover these possibilities can best be illustrated by studying how one group learned to use the sound feature of the phone. This group came to use sound files in messaging routinely from the very beginning, while two other groups mainly used text and photographs, and only occasionally sent sound files. How was it that only one group learned this possibility through small discoveries, given that sound enriched multimedia considerably (see Frohlich 2004)?

The group had eleven members. Seven members received their phones on Wednesday, June 26, 2002, but the rest had to wait until Monday, July 1. The first use of sound files happened on the evening of June 26, when Tiina sent a smiley graph from the templates of the phone to Johan and Miriam, telling in 12 seconds of audio: "it is so nice to play with this new phone. Just hope that I learn to use it. That would be a really great thing. Have a nice summer evening, ciao ciao." The next day, she sent a postcard-like audiophotograph of a lake to Andy, and received another audiophotograph from Thomas, who took a photograph of his face, saying (jokingly): "Hi, I am Thomas." She responded to him with an affectionate photograph of her face, adding kissing-like sounds and moans, thus treating his message as something akin to a courting ritual. A few minutes later, Tiina sent the kissing picture to five people in the group. Thus, by the end of the second day, she had introduced the art of audio picturing to everyone who had received the phone on June 26.

Meanwhile, something else was taking place. Thomas sent an audiophotograph of his face to his godchild, with a scary "Boo::" sound. On Saturday he received a message from Andy wondering in audio whether he had had any luck on his fishing trip. In the evening, Thomas responded to Andy with a photograph of a campfire. The audio added a camping song in duet with another, unidentifiable person. The next message to him came from Tiina, who sent a riddle from "Silja pub," asking what is in her glass. Thomas's response to her was another song, a jingle from a TV advertisement (see Messages 7.6–7.7).

As this discussion suggests, even in the very first days, people used sound in multiple ways. The next few days introduced several other uses for sound. The first significant addition came in the following week, when Ari got his hands on a multimedia phone. His audio messages almost completely consisted of cries of various sorts. His first audio message on Monday, July 1, included an image of his laughing face with loud laughter as an attachment. Another addition came when Leena started to use audio as a substitute for long text messages (in MMS). The first audio files lasted less than 10 seconds, but she later introduced others to longer messages that often lasted more than 30 seconds. Leena also started the practice of dramatizing ordinary scenery with messages using sound techniques drawn from modern media. An example of how media genres were used in sound is in Message 12.2, which borrows its format from gossip columns. It was her whispery, secretive voice that made it exciting. It would have been hard to convey such excitement in text.

This group was unique in its use of audio. In other groups, only occasional messages with sound were sent, and this aspect of mobile multimedia never grew into a culture. However, it is important to note that not all messages in the group focused on here contained audio. In fact, only about 22 percent of messages in this group during the first week contained audio. As with riddles analyzed earlier, this audio culture was a short-lived occurrence that lasted only about two weeks in our five-week study. Still, in the group studied in this section, the use of audio grew into a culture in which everyone participated in one way or another. Hence,

Message 12.2
Paparazzi

Leena_toMari
Text:br: me

01	(2.0)
02 Leena:	( ) (breaking ne—) krh Sorry *I'm
03	sorry* (whispers)
03	*test test* D'you hear me
04	Breaking news from Högbacka .hhh
05	Two celebrities have been spotted on
06	the jetty. .hh A bottle of cognac has
06	changed /ha\nds, but I couldn't get
07	a picture of it.
07	.hhh Do you recognize them.
08	(2.0)
09	*Jan Virta (0.5) Ari Mäkih* (0.5) with their
10	fami*lies.* (0.3) *and some other people,*
11	(1.0)
12	*I'll con— continue with a follow—up. h*
13	*An update soon follows.* (0.3)14 /Hi\:.

although Tiina can be held largely responsible for "inventing" audio, she was the driving force in audio messaging for only a few days. As this group developed an audio culture, members also came to use the sound function in ways other groups did not. The culture was born in interaction, and it lived as long as people used sound files in interaction.

Conclusions

Do people develop new habits when they start to use new technologies, as some have suggested (see Hosokawa 1984; Kasesniemi 2003; Lorente et al. 2002), or do they just resort to "age-old practices," sticking to old, well-known procedures and methods, as suggested by others (see Taylor and Harper 2002; du Gay et al. 1997; Miller and Slater 2000)?

This Chapter has pursued this question by studying how in three cases, small discoveries grew into more stable methods of social action. In *Mobile Image*, the pilot group created a lively image manipulation culture, while in *Radiolinja*, two such cultures were created. One group discovered the joys of riddles, while another group discovered the sound function. In both studies, these cultures were based initially on a series of discoveries in individual messages. Once these stable methods of action were established, people who participated in them had access to these more complex forms in constructing riddles, sounds, and manipulated images. However, in all three cases, people created these cultures within a spate of a couple of weeks, and continued to explore new forms of expression for a couple of weeks before going back to more common resources typical of snapshot photography (Chalfen 1987), media genres, and various age-old practices (Taylor and Harper 2002).

Chapter 3 introduced the notion of "the modification of gestalt contexture," meaning instances in which a response to a prior message places it into a new frame that transforms its meaning in surprising ways. In this Chapter, we have seen that this is one way in which discoveries take place. Such gestalt modifications take place once in a while in multimedia messages, but they seldom lead to more permanent changes in action, usually only when they become shared. That is, they become permanent when others start to experiment with these new gestalts and begin to use them regularly in their exchanges. Many if not most creative gestalt-reorganizing acts remain isolated instances of individual creativity. However, they do not have to remain isolated; they hold potential for longer-lasting changes, but only if recipients treat them as something worth trying. As the analysis of the riddle culture demonstrates, discoveries also take place when no gestalt modifications take place. Discoveries also take place within Taylor and Harper's (2002) age-old practices. Through small discoveries, people may also come to discover ways to use less obvious technical features of the device, as this Chapter has shown in analyzing sound.

Thus, this Chapter demonstrates that people make discoveries even in ordinary, age-old practices like riddles, and come to develop more elaborate ways of utilizing these practices in action over time. This argument applies more generally. Just as people discover practices like image manipulation, riddles, and sounds, there is no reason to doubt that they will make discoveries about how to utilize photographic practices and media genres for communication as well. The difference between less conspicuous discoveries (like the riddle culture in *Radiolinja*) and the more elaborate ones (like the image manipulation culture in *Mobile Image*) is one of degree. Thus, the question posed at the beginning of this Chapter, whether users are creative or not, is ultimately a matter of "granularity," how closely the analyst is willing to look at what is going on in the data. By respecifying the notion of creativity in terms of social action rather than in individual acts, one can study creativity as an observable phenomenon.

Part V

Conclusions, Data, and Methods

13

Mobile Multimedia as Ordinary Activity

Following Garfinkel (1996, 2002), Button has characterized ethnomethodology as an alternate sociology, which aims to "respecify" order in ordinary society. Following this policy, social actions are "irreducibly events in a social order and they cannot therefore be adequately identified independently of the social order in which they are embedded." The social order in which actions are sited cannot be itself identified independently of the actions themselves (Button 1993: 7). Following the policy of respecification, this volume becomes a sustained attempt to respecify mobile multimedia as an element of the social order. It has also tried to show how this very order takes shape when people are using their devices.

At the beginning of Chapter 3, I included a famous quote from Harold Garfinkel's *Studies in Ethnomethodology* (1967: vii), where Garfinkel states that in contrast to most sociological analyses, ethnomethodology's topic is the organized activities of everyday life. What Émile Durkheim called "social facts" are for Garfinkel ongoing accomplishments. For example, while for statistical purposes it makes sense to classify people by gender, Garfinkel's interest is rather in how gender is accomplished. For example, he studied how certain people come to acquire biographies typical to women and men (see Garfinkel's [1967] analysis of "Agnes").

From this perspective, my focus is on how messages are designed for communication and what recipients do with them. Although any single element in multimedia is open to many interpretations if analyzed in isolation, this is not the case in actual messages. As we have seen, multimedia elements define each other: for example, text may pick up elements from images, explaining what is significant in them. Throughout this book, we have seen that people design their messages methodically so that others understand them without difficulty. Again, this is what classic ethnomethodology leads us to expect. Senders design their multimedia messages so that they are accountable—that is, so that they appear understandable, meaningful, and orderly for recipients (Garfinkel 1967: 1). This is the basis of order in ordinary life: if someone does ordinary actions with odd methods, others would not understand what he or she is up to. As Garfinkel's "breaching experiments" (1967) have demonstrated, in such situations, others think that normality has been breached. Such an action would be seen as a joke, as an indication of bad sportsmanship, or even as an insult. In any case, the recipient(s) would be bewildered. In the worst case, others would lose their trust in the person's ability to act in a predictable, rational way.

Thus, even though action is always unique, designed on a message-by-message basis, it is remarkably stable. People take pains to ensure that their action makes sense for themselves and for other people. As these Chapters have amply demonstrated, there is "order at all points" (Sacks 1984: 22). Often, even an outsider can easily see what this order is, as in the case of the *Lammassaari Murder Story* (Message 4.5). In fact, it may be so easy to see order that it becomes unnoticeable simply because it can be taken for granted.

Ethnomethodology leads us to analyze technology through what people do with it. How technology works and develops cannot be analyzed in isolation from action; action and technology are paired. Things like technology, which are usually taken as structures (in the sense that people experience them as external factors beyond their control) become possible elements of action, not necessities that drive it from behind. It follows from this basic idea that factors typically treated as structural forces in sociology are only so if people make them somehow relevant and consequential (see Schegloff 1992a: 196; 1992b). For example, in interviews parties typically stick to questions and answers and thus "play" their roles. If an interviewer veers off this course, a politician may reprimand him, asking the interviewer to focus on his job. This is how a contextual description, the interviewee's role, becomes internal to action (see Schegloff 1992b: 116–127).

At a slightly more complex level, such structural issues may become consequential for action in how turns in talk are allocated, as in the news interview, in which the "roles" of the interviewer and the interviewee are clear at the outset in the allocation of leads, questions, answers, and who sets the course of the interview (see Drew and Hegitage 1992). Explaining order by gender, family relations, or the notion of situation would mix causes and effects, use as resource what ought to be taken as the topic of analysis. This is specifically avoided in classic ethnomethodology. It is possible to analyze these structural aspects of society in analysis, but one has to show how they are relevant in concrete actions—for instance, in ways in which agenda-setting turns and interruptions are distributed between genders.

Following the policy of respecification, this book becomes not a study of technology, nor an attempt to explain how people use it in terms of their position in society. The driving principle of analysis has been the policy that technology gets constituted in these small, ordinary acts like questions and answers, invitations and refusals, and parodies of Hollywood stories rather than on the drawing boards of engineers and designers.

Explication, not Explanation

As the very word "respecification" suggests, the nature of explanation in ethnomethodology differs from the causal thinking that characterizes much traditional sociological thinking. Studies that follow ethnomethodological principles are interested in *explicating* the orderly character of ordinary settings and activities rather than trying to explain them by establishing causal relationships or even correlations between independent and dependent variables. As Sharrock and Button note:

> If...ethnomethodology eschews the fundamental commitment to explanatory theorizing, what alternative is available? The substantial burden of its work is, we maintain, *explicatory*. Explication, though, surely means the spelling out of that which is already known, so is ethnomethodology only in the business of telling people what they already "know," repeating back to them their common-sense understandings?... The determination to identify "common-sense understandings" is not meant to result in reiteration of those understandings for their own sake, but in a context which gives a *more perspicuous view* of their part in everyday activities. (Sharrock and Button 1993: 167)

As Crabtree (2003: 73-75) has recently pointed out, ethnomethodology has affinities to the philosopher Gilbert Ryle's notion of thick description. In an influential text, Clifford Geertz (1973) has popularized this notion as an attempt to describe the "webs of meaning," but this is not what Ryle aimed at. If we follow Crabtree, Ryle was interested in describing action by thickening its description in a very specific way through a series of "accomplishment levels." Since Crabtree's interest is in describing action at the workplace, there is no need to go into detail here. Suffice to say, however, that if we follow the policy of thick description, we must not only describe what takes place in multimedia messages, but also at least three accomplishment levels: how messages are designed out of multimedia elements (Chapters 4-6), how they are embedded in social action, which typically takes a sequential form (Chapters 7-9), and how these messages come to have consequences on social organization (Chapters 10-12).

This tactic leads to some desirable theoretical consequences. In particular, it leads to "symmetrical" explanations of technology (see Bijker 1995). Both technological successes and failures are explained by the same principles, as both have their origins in ordinary activities.

Elaborating the Explication

What do we learn about mobile multimedia messaging when we follow the policy of respecification? Ultimately, the justification of any framework lies in two factors: what kinds of answers it provides to research questions and how well it performs in comparison to alternative frameworks. This section looks at the first issue, while the next section considers the second.

Chapter 1 set three questions for this book. The main question was to describe how people use mobile multimedia messages in their ordinary activities. This question was broken down into two sub-questions: how people design multimedia messages, and how they use them to interact with each other. Chapters 4-6 described the ways in which people design mobile multimedia messages using forms borrowed from snapshot photography (Chalfen 1987), media genres, and ordinary, "age-old" practices (Taylor and Harper 2002). It also described how people use sounds and bodies in designing messages. Throughout, we saw that people have at their disposal many formats for organizing messages and designing them for interaction. These Chapters have demonstrated that multimedia messaging is a skillful, even artful, and always mindful activity. People render things in their environment—what that means depends on who we are talking about—visible and communicable with their devices in an orderly manner.

While Chapters 4 and 5 focused on the internal organization of messages, Chapters 7 through 9 turned to the second sub-question, how people interact through mobile multimedia, taking their cue from the first studies of mobile multimedia (Koskinen et al. 2002) and text messaging (Kasesniemi 2003; Laursen 2005). Among other issues, I studied how people design messages so that they are understandable and justifiable, how they are replied to and responded to by recipients, and what people do to close messaging. These Chapters showed that for the most part, multimedia messaging consists of brief rather than more prolonged sequences of action. Much like ordinary conversation (Sacks et al. 1974), mobile multimedia in daily life has a "local" organization. That is, it is organized on a message-by-message basis. With the main exception of travelogues and stories, there is little evidence of longer sequences at work (see Sacks 1995, II: 354–359; Jefferson 1988).

The second question took us beyond sequential analysis. Here the aim was to study whether multimedia changes society and how such change may take place. In Kenneth Gergen's (2006) terms, is it simply another technology that splits the civil society into small monadic clusters that increasingly take on the role previously played by face-to-face conversation in public venues? How does mobile multimedia function in relation to "larger" society and its institutions such as politics, economy, religion, or art?

These questions were taken up in Chapters 10 and 11, which described some social and political uses of multimedia phones. As these Chapters demonstrated, there is little evidence of openly political uses of multimedia phones. In multimedia, politics (and other social institutions) becomes a matter of off-hand commentary rather than something serious that drives society (see Rheingold 2003a: 157–160; Pertierra et al. 2002: 101–124; Dányi and Sükösd 2003). However, there are traces of political ideology at work in a few places. Perhaps more than anything, such traces of ideology can be found in the female group in *Mobile Image*. In messages sent by these women, there were off-hand commentaries on issues such as alienation in society and the Third World, as well as criticism of technology, often in an indirect form through art or some personal involvement in political activism. As these women were students of sociology, it is possible to see them as evidence of what politically active people will do with mobile multimedia. Partly due to their theoretical training, they see, observe, and report different situations than men-on-the-street. We will no doubt see political uses of multimedia technology in the future. Thus, the main outcome of the analysis of this book must be that people use mobile multimedia mainly to entertain each other (Rivière 2005; Scifo 2005; Koskinen 2007a).

Grounded Genres and Hybrid Practices as Alternative Explanations

The second test for whether the ethnomethodology framework aids us in understanding how multimedia is used is to compare this framework to existing alternatives. By now, there are several studies of mobile multimedia devices, which have built on several theoretical frameworks. How does the framework proposed in this volume fare in comparison to these proposals?

Ling and Julsrud (2005) tried to analyze multimedia messaging in terms of "grounded genres" like postcards and documenting. As such, this framework is in many ways analogous to the ethnomethodological framework elaborated in this book. However, from the ethnomethodological framework, genre analysis has several problems, especially if it is extended to ordinary action. The first problem is that this framework does not pay enough attention to all the aspects of order available in multimedia messages. For example, how do we account for teases and counter-teases as responses to postcards? The second problem relates to analytic imagination. If we describe action as genres, we assume that genres somehow guide action from behind: people are made into what Garfinkel (1967: 69–70) called "cultural dopes."

Another available alternative framework is a somewhat syncretic attempt to analyze emergent, hybrid practices with camera phones in the context of social and cultural structures. This view, mainly proposed by Okabe and Ito in a series of papers (Okabe and Ito 2004, 2006; Okabe 2004; Ito 2005), takes as its starting point the practices of camera phone use. Okabe and Ito analyze how people interact with their devices and also the ways in which people interact with each other through them. However, unlike the ethnomethodological policy followed in this book, which focuses on the immediate context, they continue to analyze these practices in the context of social structures and cultural meanings. For example, in their analysis, "personal archiving"—like taking pictures of the covers of interesting books for future use—can be linked to how couples construct their relationships with each other in Japan by taking pictures that function as *omamori*, good luck amulets typical of mobile telephony in that country. For Okabe and Ito, practices are hybrids of actual, situated use, social structures, and cultural structures (Okabe and Ito 2006).

In theoretical terms, both grounded genres and hybrid practices can be understood as special cases of ethnomethods. For example, when we pay attention to hybrid practices, we may see slight modifications in the methods people employ when designing action. Ito (2005), for example, has rightly pointed out, couples may truncate multimedia messages into mere visual reports instead of using the more explicit forms typical for acquaintances. For couples, the important thing is the very act of being in touch. In that work, they no doubt use cultural structures such as omamori to give shape to their thoughts. It may be that this analysis will lead to important insights in the future and help connect ethnomethodological analysis to cultural and social structures. However, saying that it has already done so would be an overstatement. At the moment, Okabe and Ito's work is in its early stages, and has not yet been elaborated enough to be evaluated fairly. The same observation is also true of Scifo's (2005) analysis, which has structuralist overtones.

For several reasons, it is difficult to evaluate the pros and cons of these alternative methodologies fairly. They are typically not elaborated theoretically. Also, these perspectives have not been tested systematically with large data sets. For instance, it is apparent that Ito (2005) is right when she observes that couples send meaningless messages just to maintain "visual co-presence": couples do send visual updates of their whereabouts, apparently just to keep each other in their minds. However, perceptive as her analysis is, it is based on two couples only. It thus serves as a useful deviant case to Koskinen's (2005a) analysis of messaging between acquaintances, but it is difficult to generalize her analysis any further. For example, is it possible to use this framework to interpret jokes between colleagues?

These remarks point out the importance of theoretical debate. In the final analysis, it is only possible to point out problems in any proposed theoretical framework by crafting clearly stated arguments that can be refuted. In hoping to engender such debate, the proposal made in this book is modest, meant to serve as a preliminary rather than definitive statement about mobile multimedia.

Is Mobile Multimedia Juvenile?: Limits of Explication

A referee of this book characterized its pictures as "juvenile." To a large extent, this observation is true. On the pages of this book, the reader has seen images that would certainly not be shot by a grandmother or a serious politician. However, to see the implications of the referee's observation, we need to distinguish two questions.

The first concerns the nature of the data. For several reasons, these data did have a juvenile character. The case of *Mobile Image* was obvious. As Table 14.1 shows, the people in that study were young urban dwellers. The case of *Radiolinja* is slightly more complicated. In that study, the oldest participants were in their mid-thirties, and the average age of the second group was over thirty when the study began (see Table 14.2). However, this group cannot be said to be old by any standard; most of its members were married, though few had young children. Also, the study took place during the vacation season in July, which probably explains the fact that leisurely, jocular activities characterize the data.

It is difficult to compare these data to other bodies of data for methodological reasons. However, Okabe and Ito (2004, 2006) provide examples of images from Tokyo and Banks et al. (2002) from London. These images resemble the Finnish data in many ways, which suggests that when young people get access to camera phones, they use them to capture things that may be meaningful for them, but not necessarily for more mature audiences. Of course, it is possible that more senior people will capture things that are relevant for them. However, it may also be that there is something in the device that makes it suitable for capturing intuitively odd, funny, beautiful, or shocking things. If that is the case, then even more mature people may use their phones to capture "juvenile" things rather than the more traditional objects of the Kodak culture (Chalfen 1987). Only time and future studies will tell. Nevertheless, with the present data, a word of caution must be raised.

The second question concerns the institutional grounds of action. Several studies suggest that if multimedia phones are used in institutional action, they are used differently from ordinary action. One study in particular is important in this respect. In their study of how three occupational groups use multimedia phones, Ling and Julsrud describe not only the uses of carpenters, soft drink salespersons, and real estate agents, but also note that there are significant differences in the ways these groups use the devices. The actual differences notwithstanding, the important point for us is that Ling and Julsrud's observations suggest that at work, people may use multimedia phones to support occupationally specific forms of reasoning, whether conceptual or visual (see also Koskinen et al. 2002: 98–101).

As Chapter 10 suggests, this may also be the case with, say, political activists. When one is engaged in political action, one learns to see and communicate things in a new light. If camera phones are used as tools in political action, pictures and their textual and audio rim surely may differ from what we have seen in this book. However, this is not necessarily the case. As Ling and Julsrud also observed, in real estate agents' hands, multimedia was used mainly for social rather than occupational purposes, perhaps reflecting the fact that this occupation is known for cut-throat competition and disloyalty rather than for buddy spirit and free exchange of information. Also, although camera phone pictures have been published in quality newspapers (Noguchi 2005; Dunleavy 2005), journalists seem to use their cameras almost exactly in the same way as ordinary people. Texts, too, resemble what we have seen on the pages of this book: they are typically amusing and often sarcastic comments on items in photographs (see Margolis 2005).

Thus, mobile multimedia may, and no doubt will, maintain institutional forms of action, not only those juvenile forms that have their ground in immediate, ordinary life. Future studies must focus on institutional contexts rather than on action only. Theoretically, this observation opens a new line of analysis that can best be clarified by an analogy to talk and conversation. In conversation analysis, it is customary to distinguish ordinary conversation from institutional talk (see Drew and Heritage 1992). The latter borrows its basic forms from ordinary conversation (Sacks et al. 1974), but uses more limited, but elaborated forms that are specifically designed to keep work possible and going (Heritage 1989). In these terms, this book has focused on ordinary action, trying to explicate what kinds of orientations keep it going. Thus, when reading this book one has to keep in mind its limitations; just as the referee suggested, it is ultimately about how the young urban middle class is using yet another cyber technology for sociable chit-chat.

Beyond the First Generation of Technology:
More Limits to Explication

Another possible limit concerns technology, which, unlike "age-old" human forms of action, does change rapidly. Is there something going on in technology that limits extrapolation from this study? The timing of both studies reported here took place in the pivotal early days of mobile multimedia in Europe. However, even though *Mobile Image* and *Radiolinja* come from a specific point in time and a specific context, Helsinki, Finland, with one of the most advanced mobile markets in the world, the focus on ordinary methods of action lends this book certain predictive validity. It is a safe guess that a good deal of mobile multimedia's social consequences will take place in ordinary interaction, in situations in which people send messages to each other and respond to them (for an analogous argument about the primacy of conversation, see Heritage 1989: 239–240). For example, there is no reason to think that people will change the ways in which they ask questions simply because they have access to devices with new features. This book gives tools for understanding a significant chunk of mobile multimedia in action for years to come.

Is there something in sight in technology that will change this picture? One promise of multimedia builds on its ability to make "services" visual and thus more attractive than services based on text messages or WAP (Eriksson et al. 2001; Andersson and Heinonen 2002; Teo and Pok 2003a; 2003b). The argument has a historical precedent. While the Internet was primarily an academic instrument until 1993–1994, it was the visualization brought about by the Web that introduced it to the general public. Still, the history of mobile video technology is largely a history of failures. Usability problems, security concerns and social barriers—like the visibility of the display to outsiders—will plague small devices for years to come (Schnaars 1989; Repo et al. 2003; O'Hara et al. 2006).

Another recent development is "moblogs," Web sites into which people can send multimedia messages that can then be browsed with computers and mobile phones. However, moblogging seems to be unusual even in Japan, where moblogging first took off around 2002 (Okada 2005: 49). In a recent review, Döring and Gundolf (2005) have shown that although there exist hundreds of thousands of moblogs today, relatively few are active for a long time. Rather, it appears that people experiment with them for awhile before abandoning them. It may well be that we will see a haphazard use of moblogs in the future: people set them up for special reasons—for example, to share holiday pictures while on the move—after which the sites lie unused for long periods of time before the next surge of action. As mobile phones become increasingly integrated with the Internet, some new uses will probably attract enough following to become a success. However, moblog practices are typically based on the idea of an online photo album, and are in many ways based on different types of ethnomethods other than messaging. It is a difference of a similar kind than the one between conversation and photo albums.

The big industrial question at the end of the decade was mobile TV. The first experiments in making movies for mobile phones were known as "micromovies" (see Boyd Davis 2002; Metso et al. 2004), small-scale movies that can be viewed with mobile phones and PDAs. There have even been several micromovie festivals at least in France, the United States, and Finland, and even movie prizes have been awarded to the best works in these festivals. Of course, showcases in media art do not mean success in society. With the partial exception of South Korea (Ok 2005), micromovies have been popular with a small group of technology enthusiasts and digital artists rather than with the public at large. Also, watching television is another type of activity than designing and receiving multimedia messages (Holly et al. 2001; Ayass 2006).

If a cautious prediction of the future of mobile multimedia is possible, it might look like this: mobile multimedia will continue to generate profits for handset manufacturers and mobile telephone operators, but growth in the digital content-producing industries will be much less pronounced. Age-old practices that guide people in how to use mobile multimedia change slowly, thus product development ought not to expect a sudden increase in consumers' imagination and willingness to play, pay and have fun using commercial formats. It may be that the "killer application," so eagerly sought by the mobile industry, is already here, and indeed is the same as in text messages: people use their devices to interact with others.

The Social Construction of Mobile Multimedia

Chapter 1 referred to Wiebe E. Bijker's (1995) understanding of technology. For Bijker, technology does not develop as an internal process, but its course is construed in social interaction. His unit of analysis is the sociotechnical ensemble, which is a pair of social and technical forces. Even though technical artifacts as such exhibit interpretive flexibility in that they can be interpreted in many ways—for instance, multimedia phones can be thought of as phones, text messaging machines, or cameras—this is not the case in real society, except perhaps in the case of the first years of radically new technologies. Instead, technological frames develop to guide the ways in which people understand technology and see its restrictions and possibilities. When interpretive flexibility is low, Bijker talks about "closure": after a technology has become stable, people think about it using only one fixed set of meanings.

Much as alternative proposals in the sociology of technology (Hughes 1983; Latour 1987), Bijker's analysis stresses major players like scientists, engineers, and large corporations rather than ordinary people as key stakeholders in the definitional processes. In Chapter 1, I suggested three technological frames for mobile multimedia—text messages, photographs, and audio recorders—as possible candidates for how people can make sense of this technology. We have seen that all three function as technological frames in Bijker's sense. So far, it has been the camera function that has primarily framed mobile multimedia, which may be reflected in the very term "camera phone." However, we have also seen that there is more to mobile multimedia than just technological frames: the ordinary activities people do with their devices. Although people may orient to their devices using several technological frames, these frames are only "hinges" in action rather than something that guides action in any strict sense (Bijker 1995: 194–197).

It would plainly be silly to deny the importance of handset manufacturers like Nokia, Ericsson (now SonyEricsson), Motorola, and Samsung in how mobile multimedia develops. What I am arguing here instead is that although handset manufacturers may have provided the main elements of what Bijker calls "technological frames" by combining several functions that have existed separately into one device, people also play a part in defining which elements of the frame become reality. The ways in which people use the first generation of multimedia phones sets limits on what technology companies can do in the next step. Thus, although my argument is in line with Bijker's analysis, it recasts it in ethnomethodological terms. Technological frames may be constituted by industries, but their effect on multimedia is filtered through ordinary activities. With consumer technologies like mobile multimedia, we need to give a prominent place in our analysis to what people do with these technologies. By attempting to respecify how people use these devices, we see the very thing we need to see in order to understand mobile multimedia adequately: the constitution of technology in ordinary action.

14

Data and Methods

Mobile Multimedia in Action is based on a series of studies conducted in Helsinki, Finland, between 1999 and 2002. More specifically, two studies have provided data for it: *Mobile Image* (1999–2001) and *Radiolinja* (2002), both of which were conducted at the University of Art and Design Helsinki.

At present, most studies of mobile multimedia—or camera phones— carried out by social scientists rely on traditional methods of social science, including observation, interviewing, and analysis of actual images in people's phones (see Kindberg et al. 2004). In some studies, people using camera phones have been videotaped as well (Jacucci et al. 2006). The only addition to standard methodology is the diary, which is routinely used in studies of mobile technology, but less prevalent in the social sciences. For example, using a diary-based methodology and a cultural conceptual framework, Ito and Okabe (Okabe and Ito 2004; Ito 2005; Okabe and Ito 2006) researched camera phone uses in the Tokyo-Kanto region in August–September 2003 by studying fifteen people (two high school students, eight college students, two housewives, and three professionals). They asked the participants to record several details in diaries: the time of usage; who they were in contact with; who initiated the contact; where they were; what kind of communication type was used; why they chose that form of communication; who was in the vicinity at the time; problems associated with the usage; and the content of the communication. Also, participants were asked to keep records of photos they took, received, and shared. Researchers asked people to submit the last ten pictures for research. These data were completed with interviews. More or less similar methods have been used in other studies (Scifo 2005; Kindberg et al. 2004).

In addition, in user-centered technology development, researchers have set up systems that make it possible to observe and, sometimes, collect actual messages from the Web. A group of researchers led by van House and Davis (2005) conducted a two-stage study on metadata and MMS building on activity theory and ethnomethodology. In *MMM1*, they gave MMS-capable phones to over sixty users for four months to study capturing images, finding at the end of that time that sharing is as essential as capturing. In *MMM2*, sharing was supported with a Web-based system, which used metadata of various sorts to support sharing. The main question was concerned with whom people wanted to share their pictures. *MMM2* used a pool of sixty users (forty students, twenty researchers), but this time, the trial lasted six months. Jacucci et al. (2006) studied the uses of MMS in capturing and sharing—or co-experiencing (Battarbee 2004)—"large-scale events." They studied two participant groups at the World Rally Championship Race in 2004 in Jyväskylä, a city located in central Finland. The rally is a three-day event with approximately 300,000 spectators. Researchers gave eight multimedia phones to two groups, one consisting of seven men in their early thirties, recruited from a small town. Another group consisted of three men and one woman, who were recruited from the Helsinki region. They were instructed to use the phones, and told to save all material, but no other instructions were given. During the rally, researchers "shadowed" (a sociologist would say "observed") the users with a video camera. After the rally, the cameras were collected, and the videos and photographs were extracted for analysis.

Although there is a fast-growing body of literature on mobile multimedia by now, there were few features to build on when *Mobile Image* started in 1999. For this study, my colleagues and I created a methodology that was based on collecting messages that people actually send to each other. The system was based on using the Web as an observational instrument in ways that are explained below. It was originally developed for *Mobile Image*, but we used a similar, though more advanced procedure in *Radiolinja*. The benefits in collecting actual messages are many: we see messaging from the member's point of view, as something that takes place in actual interaction. We also have access to exact timings in messages, and know exactly to whom messages were sent—and can thus cross-check claims made in interviews. (Koskinen et al. 2005b).

With this method, however, we are not aware of the circumstances in which photographs were captured, but we do have access to perhaps the most important chunk of multimedia experience, the actual message. Also, in many cases, we can determine fully how the message is understood by the recipients. We have access to this context as formulated by the senders. Notice that this *is* the way in which this context appears to people who use multimedia phones. The recipient cannot experience smell, noise, wind, unless they are explained in the message; the recipient's response cannot be based on what he does not know. In turn, the sender does not know the recipient's inner thoughts unless they are formulated in the response. With our methodology, we are able to study interaction as it evolves, and although this is not a perfect methodology for studying, say, the live work of capture (see Salovaara and Jacucci 2006), it provides us with a firm ground for analyzing an important chunk of multimedia, as it appears in interaction for the sender and the recipient when they are communicating with each other.

Design Studies as Data

It is important to bear in mind that the data for this book come from a series of design studies that were done when the technology was in an early stage, at a time when research was still capable of informing design. The aim was to create a rich picture of how people would use technology that was not yet on the market. Of course, there is no way to know whether uses described in this book will become common. Still, the choice of the method responds primarily to that need. As Ling and Julsrud (2005) note elsewhere, in 1999–2002, mobile multimedia was too small an issue to be studied with standard quantitative research methods. A better option was to conduct a series of field studies in which several groups of people were given access to technology, but little guidance about how they should use it, and then follow evolving usage.

There are some obvious problems in this approach. Results are constrained by technology and, secondly, by some solutions and activities of the researchers. Also, when researchers provide people with technical help, it is impossible to know how difficulties in actual technology and its usability will shape usage in the future. Studying groups instead of individual people poses its own set of problems as well. These groups may be too close-knit, or just develop unique cultures that are creations of the moment rather than anything long-lasting. In none of these studies did we try to cover all age groups or socioeconomic levels equally, as it would have been impossible to gather fully representative data for reasons of time and limited equipment.

However, as our focus has been on actual methods of use, these limitations do not pose significant problems. Interaction is a funny thing.

Regardless of gender, age, situation, or political opinion, simply to live not only people have to ask questions and get them answered, return greetings and, should they like to present riddles to others, build them using certain methods to ensure that recipients understand what is going on. This understanding is a precondition for smooth action. We are dealing with the methods of Durkheimian "immortal ordinary society," as Garfinkel (1996, 2002) formulates it. These practices will remain largely the same, although new technologies and the increased sophistication of users may bring some changes and modifications later on.

Mobile Image

In the first study, *Mobile Image*, done with industrial designer Esko Kurvinen and sociologist Turo-Kimmo Lehtonen, we gave a Nokia Communicator (9110) and a Casio digital camera to four groups for roughly two months each to be used freely. Telephone service was provided by Radiolinja (today Elisa), a Helsinki-based mobile operator. In 1999, the Communicator was the only phone on the market capable of storing, sending, and receiving photographs. With the Casio camera, people could take pictures, beam them into the phone with infrared, and send them as attachments in e-mail messages. Recipients could view these messages either in e-mail, or download them to their phones to be viewed on the screen, which used gray-scale colors at that time. The whole process took place over a wireless connection (GSM).

The four groups of the study were chosen with gender being a central criterion for selection. Gender, training in the visual arts or photography, and technological fluency were key selection criteria, with age, area of residence, and occupation being less important. Most participants lived in the Helsinki metropolitan area, were either students or recent graduates, and were typically in their late twenties or early thirties. We opened e-mail accounts and created access for all participants in the computer system of the University of Art and Design Helsinki to make sure that the technology worked.

Each group attended a two-hour training session arranged at the Department of Product and Strategic Design, which concentrated on how to use the camera and the Communicator. We ensured that the features and functions essential for our experiment were introduced and that members had a chance to practice them. In addition, we alerted the subjects to a couple of www. albums (mainly Zing). The Communicators were prepared in advance.

Table 14.1
Groups in *Mobile Image*

1. Pilot group: 30.6.1999—31.12.2000
   Researchers of the University of Art and Design Helsinki, four men and one
   woman (three industrial designers, two sociologists) (*1961–1973)
2. Male group: 2.3.—8.5.2000
   A group of friends, university-level business and engineering students/
   graduates already in jobs (*1973–1975)
3. Female group: 17.5—3.7.2000
   A group of friends, students of social sciences at the University of Helsinki
   (*1973–1976)
4. Control group: 14.12.2000—15.3.2001
   Friends and work acquaintances, designers working in a U.S.-owned new
   media company (training in design and technology)(*1977–1979)

Note: Pseudonyms are used in text when we refer to these people. Names are changed
each time to hide their identities.

Figure 14.1
Images in Messages by Week in Two Groups of *Mobile Image*

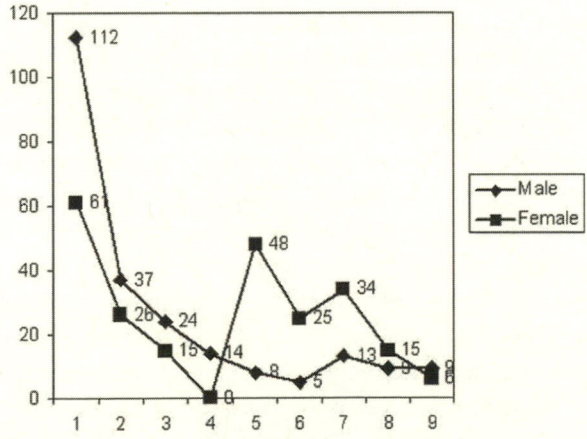

Visual material was collected as e-mail attachments. Every Communicator had the e-mail addresses and phone numbers of the participants pre-installed, so sending a photograph to the entire group was possible with a single dial command. Esko Kurvinen's e-mail address was added to this list. In addition, we requested that when the participants sent photographs to people outside the research group, they would simultaneously send the photograph to Kurvinen (Figure 14.1).

Our material was supplemented by two personal interviews of each participant. The initial interview focused on the participant's computer and photography experience and/or photography hobby. This initial interview brought up some differences between and within the groups, the most significant being related to image-processing experience and the extent of IT experience and skills. Experience in photography varied from beginner to a relatively serious amateur. The final interview focused on the experiment itself and what took place during it. The participants were asked about their experiences using the equipment and for their interpretations of what had taken place. The visual messages sent by the group were numbered and discussed in the final interviews. In the interviews, photographs were referred to by numbers. This enabled us to trace references that came up in the interviews to specific photographs, which made it possible to interpret the interviews with precision. Esko Kurvinen carried out the interviews.

For the most part, I have used data from the male and female groups, although I have also used in the text some examples from the pilot and control groups. During the experiment the male and the female groups sent a total of 371 e-mail messages (258+113). A single message contained 1–16 photographs. Although the female group sent only half as many messages as the male group, the messages they sent contained a larger sum total of photographs. Especially towards the end of the experiment, both male and female group members tended to include several photographs in a single message. There is another interesting feature about the graph depicting communication in the female group, as it shows how social the communication was. For example in week four of the experiment, not a single photograph was sent (partly because of technical problems). In week five, dozens of photographs were sent, partly as a response to the log gathered during the previous, quiet week. Sending photographs was episodic and again speaks to the reciprocal nature of social activity: when one member sent a photograph, the others had an incentive to send similar images.

Radiolinja

The Radiolinja MMS Study (called *Radiolinja* in this book) was done with industrial designers Esko Kurvinen and Katja Battarbee and several assistants. In *Radiolinja*, we followed three user groups in the Finnish mobile phone operator Radiolinja's (now Elisa) technology and service pilot, which took place July 11–20, 2002, and lasted about five weeks. Three mixed-gender groups with seven, eleven, and seven members were studied. There were fifteen men and ten women in these groups. The average age was 28 (Md=30).

As in *Mobile Image*, each user was given a multimedia phone. Seventeen participants had Nokia 7650 with an integrated camera, and eight SonyEricsson T68i with a plug-in camera. Out of the *Radiolinja* pilot, we selected groups to take into account gender difference, terminal types, and the city-countryside axis. Most participants lived in the Helsinki metropolitan area, though exact details about these groups are confidential. Figure 14.2. describes the weekly frequencies of messages.

Exact numbers of messages are confidential, but the following figures point to the scale of messaging in the pilot. In all, users sent over 4,000 messages during the pilot. Over 2,000 of those messages were unique (the rest being duplicates in group messages, or recycled messages). These data were produced through the Radiolinja system automatically. The service was free of charge for the participants.

Table 14.2
Groups in *Radiolinja*

1. Group: 30.6.1999—31.12.2000
     Seven members, who knew each other in the beginning. Average age in the beginning of the study 22 years (*1967–1981)
2. Group: 2.3.—8.5.2000
     Eleven members, who knew each other in the beginning. Average age in the beginning of the study 31 years (*1965–1972)
3. Group: 17.5—3.7.2000
     Seven members, who knew each other in the beginning. Average age in the beginning of the study 27 years (*1972–1979)

Note: Pseudonyms are used in text when we refer to these people. Names are changed each time to hide their identities.

Figure 14.2
Frequency of Messaging in *Radiolinja* (first 5 weeks)

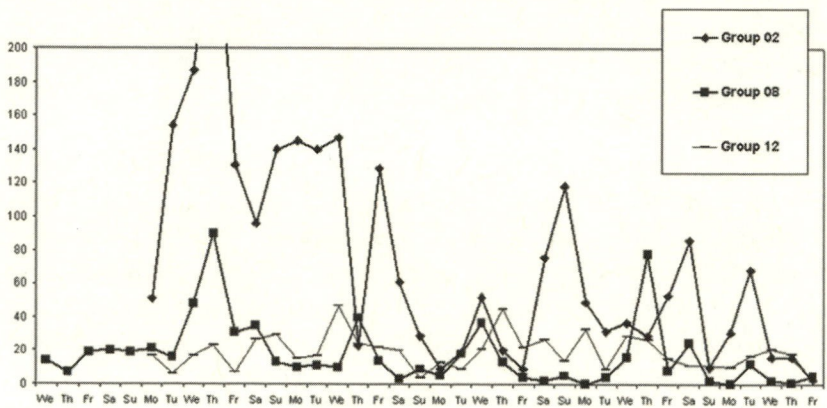

For this book, I have treated these data in the following fashion. From the vast mass of *Radiolinja* messages, I chose a subsample consisting of 543 messages, sent by the first group (with seven members) during the third and fourth weeks and by the second group (eleven members) during the fourth week of the study. Analysis started from this set; its structure is explained later in this Chapter. Transcription of the audio data follows the conventions of conversation analysis (Table 14.3).

To analyze sound, I randomly selected week four of Group three for analysis. This sample resulted in a set of seventy-two audio messages, that is, files with an audio component. However, most of these were sent as copies: only fourteen are original, the rest, like the baby example (Message 5.4), were sent up to ten persons. The length of the audio clips ranged from 4 seconds to slightly over 30 seconds. With the exception of one graphic, there was always a photograph in the message. Three messages were sent without text. There were twenty-eight distinguishable ambient audio elements in these data. In ten cases, these elements were ambient noise: sounds of shopping malls, the street and bars, but also wind, echo and radio in the background. In eighteen cases, human sounds were in an ambient role. In twelve cases, there was indistinguishable talk in the background, in five cases laughter, and in one case a crying baby.

Table 14.3
Transcript Symbols (adapted from Jefferson 1984)

(.)	Micropause, or interval of 0.1 second in talk.
(0.4)	An interval of 0.4 seconds.
'n [she sa]id [But th-]	Overlap begins and ends.
=[[I'm saying [[But no::	Utterances start simultaneously.
Wha:t	A colon indicates an extension of the sound it follows. Each colon is about 0.1 seconds.
.	A period indicates a stopping fall in tone.
,	A comma indicates a slight fall in tone.
?	A question mark indicates a rising inflection.
?,	A combined question mark/comma indicates a slight rising intonation.
;	Continuous intonation.
/ \	Rise and fall in intonation
Wha:t	Underlining indicates emphasis.
WHAT	Loudly.
what	Quietly, or in whisper.
hhh .hhh .nhh	Outbreath, inbreath, and inbreath through nose respectively. Each "h" is about 0.1 seconds.
(what)( ) say	Single parentheses indicate transcriber's doubt or best guess.
((door slams))	Double parentheses indicate various features of the setting or transcriber's comments.
.mt .pt	Click or a smack of tongue, and the same in English.
.nff	Snuffling.
#that's true#	Creaky voice.
@what@	Markedly different tone than elsewhere.
$wht's th't$	Laughing voice.
W(h)hat	Within words, (h) is a laughter token.
He HEHEH ha	Laughter tokens.
wh—	Cutoff of a word.
And th( )<	The speaker halts some unit in progress.
>she said<	Quickly.

Analysis

It would be impossible to analyze a data mass of almost 5,000 messages in detail. For this reason, I followed the principles of analytic induction. This procedure starts with generating hypotheses from data, which are then tested until the designer has an interpretation that describes the data thoroughly. Analytic induction has five steps (comp. Seale 1999; Koskinen et al. 2005a):

1. In the first phase, a small number of cases (here mobile multimedia messages) is analyzed closely, pushing hunches and inspiration too far. At this stage, it is important to be creative. Unworthy ideas are dismissed later.
2. The second stage is to create a set of hypotheses from this analysis.
3. In the third stage, these hypotheses are tested with these same data.
4. When a hypothesis stands this preliminary test, the analysis proceeds to deviant cases that fit the emerging hypothesis only with difficulty. If the case does not fit the hypothesis, the hypothesis is discarded, revised, or new dimensions are added to the analysis. Analysis proceeds until all cases have been analyzed, and there is a description that describes all data. Typically, this is a conceptual framework that is ordered from the most important concepts to the less important ones. This conceptual framework can simply be called "an interpretation."
5. Up to this point, only a subset of data has been used, and there is no way of knowing whether this interpretation is correct in all data. Thus, there is a final step, generalizing the interpretation with all the data that have been gathered.

Mobile Image was treated as a pilot study in which a set of hypotheses was created in order to analyze the data from *Radiolinja*. This was because although *Mobile Image* dealt with what are perhaps the key multimedia elements, image and text, the sound function was missing, and its technology was far more difficult to use than in actual multimedia phones in 2002 when *Radiolinja* was carried out.

Analyzing *Radiolinja* data proceeded as follows. After posing a research question for each Chapter (for example, how do people design messages in the opening position? Chapter 7) or subsection in a Chapter (for instance, what kinds of riddles are there?), the first analytic phase was to search for a collection of cases. When a collection of cases was created, the analysis continued with an unmotivated search of similarities and recurrent issues. When a hypothesis arose—for example, I described the structure of riddles—I treated it as a working model, which I then tested with all the data in the collection, actively searching for negative cases. When such cases were found, its status was decided, and the working model reworked. In the case of riddles, for example, this procedure led to the realization that riddles are typically extended with clues and an evaluation phase.

This procedure is time-consuming and can be cumbersome, but it has its virtues. A good interpretation typically has a few clear and distinct concepts, which are related to each other in a systematic fashion. Importantly, this procedure also starts from the data, so analytic work focuses on actual messages instead of theoretical concepts. This book includes about eighty actual messages and forty or more are mentioned in the text. The argument is developed through actual examples, which also provide readers with the possibility to disagree, as they can point out details that are missing from the analysis. The aim of the procedure is to create understanding, not to push the audience into a sea of meaningless details. Methodologist Abraham Kaplan once crystallized the importance of focusing on the essentials with a story of a drunkard searching for his key:

> There is a story of a drunkard searching under a street lamp for his house key, which he had dropped some distance away. When asked why he didn't look where he had dropped it, he replied, "It's lighter here!" Much effort, not only in the logic of behavioral science, but also in behavioral science itself, is vitiated, in my opinion, by the principle of the drunkard's search. (Kaplan 1964: 11)

This procedure translates knowledge about the user into understanding—that is, it picks up what is essential from fuzzy intuition. What the audience gets is an economical snapshot of the user and his or her world. Such a picture is parsimonious, following Occam's razor that advises us to opt for the simpler of two competing theories. This picture may not be correct in all details, but this is not the point. What is truly important is that this picture communicates the user well to the audience, justifying the investments in time, effort, and technological know-how spent on analysis.

Research Ethics

I have followed several kinds of ethical procedures, some for legal, and some for ethical reasons. Their origins are in practices that I have followed with my colleagues over the years. In particular, in *Radiolinja*, our hands were tied by Finnish law, which protects the privacy of telecommunications. In addition, participants were informed about the study, its possible ethical problems, and about the ethical procedures we used before they consented to participate in the study. In particular, we told them how our data was produced, promised not to publish messages without their consent, and promised to change details of images so that it would not be possible to identify them in our publications. In addition, we have followed standard academic and legal practice, changing all names and details that could identify people or places.

Much like in ethnographic research (see Becker 1970: 42–44) and conversation analysis (Maynard 1984: 21–22), these precautions were barely sufficient: as several open quarrels, pornographic photographs, and plainly silly messages sent during drinking sprees revealed, people soon forgot that researchers were able to follow their messages. In selecting examples for analysis, I have tried to be tactful, respecting the privacy of participants. In selecting examples for this book, I have opted for the more ordinary messages even though in some cases—for example, in riddles—better but cruder examples would have been available.

Data for *Mobile Image* was gathered through e-mail. Since we did not gather all messages automatically, it is obvious that we have not succeeded in collecting all the messages sent. However, this was not our purpose either: for reasons of research ethics, we wanted to give our participants the option of not sending all their messages to the researchers. For this reason we did not have a system of automatically collecting the messages from the computer system of the University of Art and Design or through Radiolinja (now Elisa), the GSM-operator with which we worked.

In *Radiolinja*, we were able to follow messaging as it took place through a Web-based system used by the company in its technical pilot. We were granted the right to follow the Web site, and make a copy of its activity during the trial. However, the company owns these data, and has a right to screen our publications before they are submitted in order to check for possible mistakes in technical information, as well as to consider possible legal issues. Thus far, the *Radiolinja* project has produced about thirty scientific publications, and the company's only corrections have been on purely technical details. Finally, legal issues are important in any study of telecommunications, as they are closely protected through legal means. However, one way around this problem is to get permission from the people studied. Another way to get at actual telecommunications is through a technology pilot: in a pilot like *Radiolinja*, messages are not governed by laws on actual telecommunications. Participants were given access to technology, which was free for them; in exchange, they gave us the right to study their telecommunications.

Bibliography

Andersson, Per, and Kristina Heinonen. 2002. *Acceptance of Mobile Services. Insights from the Swedish Market for Mobile Telephony*. Stockholm: Stockholm School of Economics. SSE/EFI Working Paper Series in Business Administration No. 2002, 16.

Arminen, Ilkka. 2005. *Institutional Interaction. Studies of Talk at Work*. Aldershot: Ashgate Publishing.

Atkinson, J. Maxwell, and Paul Drew. 1979. *Order in Court. The Organisation of Verbal Interaction in Judicial Settings*. London: Macmillan.

Ayass, Ruth. 2006. Using the Remote Control. Paper presented at the International Conference on Conversation Analysis, ICCA 2006, Helsinki, May 10-14.

Banks, Harriet, Tom Vernon-Kell, Jo Jackson, and Rory Brady. 2002. *see what i'm talking about?* Espoo, Finland: Sävypaino.

Bannon, Liam. 1991. "From Human Factors to Human Actors. The Role of Psychology and Human-Computer Interaction Studies in System Design." In Greenbaum, Joan, and Morten Kyng, eds. *Design at Work. Cooperative Design of Computer Systems*. Hillsdale, NJ: Lawrence Erlbaum.

Barnes, Stuart J., and Sid L. Huff. 2003. "Rising Sun: iMode and the Wireless Internet." *Communications of the ACM* 46: 79–84.

Barry, Michael, and LiAnne Yu. 2002. "The Uses and Meaning of I-mode in Japan." *Revista de estudios de juventud* 57: 151–172.

Battarbee, Katja. 2004. *Co-Experience. Understanding User Experiences in Social Interaction*. Helsinki: University of Art and Design.

———, and Ilpo Koskinen. 2004. "Co-Experience--User Experience as Interaction." *CoDesign Journal* 1: 5–18.

Becker, Howard S. 1970. *Sociological Work. Method and Substance*. New Brunswick, NJ: Transaction Publishers.

Berg, Sara, Alex S. Taylor, and Richard Harper. 2003. "Mobile Phones for the Next Generation: Device Designs for Teenagers." *Proceedings of CHI*, Vol. 5(1) Ft. Lauderdale, Florida, April 5-10.

Bergmann, Jörg R. 1993. *Discreet Indiscretions. The Social Organization of Gossip*. New York: Aldine de Gruyter.

Bijker, Wiebe. 1995. *Of Bicycles, Bakelites, and Bulbs*. Cambridge, MA: The MIT Press.

Black, Donald. 1976. *The Behavior of Law*. New York: Academic Press.

Bourdieu, Pierre, ed. 1990. *Photography. A Middle-Brow Art*. London: Polity Press.

Boyd Davis, Stephen. 2002. "Interacting with Pictures: Film, Narrative and Personalization." *Digital Creativity* 13: 71–82.

Bradley, Steven P., and Matthew Sandoval. 2002. "NTT DoCoMo. The Future of the Wireless Internet?" *Journal of Interactive Marketing* 16: 80–96.

Bull, Michael. 2000. *Sounding Out the City*. Oxford: Berg.

Button, Graham. 1993. Introduction. In Button, Graham, ed. *Ethnomethodology and the Human Sciences*. Cambridge: Cambridge University Press.

Chalfen, Richard. 1987. *Snapshot Versions of Life*. Bowling Green, OH: Bowling Green State University Press.

Cooley, Heidi Rae. 2005. The Autobiographical Impulse and Mobile Imaging: Toward a Theory of Autobiometry. Paper presented at the Workshop Pervasive Image Capture and Sharing: New Social Practices and Implications for Technology at *Ubicomp'05*, Shinagawa, Tokyo, September 11–14. Retrieved September 20, 2005, from http://ubicomp.org/ubicomp2005.

Crabtree, Andy. 2003. *Designing Collaborative Systems. A Practical Guide to Ethnography*. London: Springer.

Dant, Tim. 2005. *Materiality and Society*. Maidenhead: Open University Press.

Dányi, Endre, and Miklós Sükösd. 2003. "M-Politics in the Making: SMS and E-Mail in the 2002 Hungarian Election Campaigns." In Nyíri, Kristóf, ed. *Mobile Communication. Essays on Cognition and Community*. Vienna: Passagen Verlag.

Darley, Andrew. 2000. *Visual Digital Culture. Surface Play and Spectacle in New Media Genres*. London: Routledge.

Drew, Paul. 1978. Accusations. "The Occasioned Use of Members' Knowledge of 'Religious Geography' in Describing Events." *Sociology* 12: 1–22.

———. 1987. "Po-Faced Receipts of Teases." *Linguistics* 25: 219–253.

———, and Elizabeth Holt. 1988. "Complainable Matters: The Use of Idiomatic Expressions in Making Complaints." *Social Problems* 35: 398–417.

———, and John Heritage. 1992. "Analysing Talk at Work: An Introduction." In Drew, Paul, and John Heritage, eds. *Talk at Work. Institutional Interaction in Institutional Settings*. Cambridge: Cambridge University Press.

du Gay, Paul, Stuart Hall, Linda Jones, Hugh Mackay, and Keith Negus. 1997. *Doing Cultural Studies. The Story of the Sony Walkman*. London: Sage.

Dunleavy, Dennis. 2005. Camera Phones Prevail: Citizen Shutterbugs and the London Bombings. July 9, 2005. Retrieved Oct. 6, 2005, from http://digitaljournalist.org/issue0507/dunleavy.html.

Döring, Nicola, Christine Dietmar, Alexandra Hein, and Katharina Hellwig. 2005. "Contents, Forms and Functions of Interpersonal Pictorial Messages in Online and Mobile Communication." In *Proceedings of Seeing, Understanding. Learning in the Mobile Age. Communications in the 21st Century: The Mobile Information Society*. Budapest, Hungary, April 28-30.

———, and Axel Gundolf. 2005. "Your Life in Snapshots: Mobile Weblogs (Moblogs)." In Glotz, Peter, Stefan Bertschi, and Chris Locke, eds. *Thumb Culture. The Meaning of Mobile Phones for Society*. Bielefeld: transcript Verlag.

Eriksson, Päivi, Kaarina Hyvönen, Anu Raijas, and Markku Tinnilä. 2001. *Mobiilipalveluiden käyttö 2001--asiantuntijoille työtä ja miehille leikkiä?* Helsinki: Kuluttajatutkimuskeskus. Työselosteita ja esitelmiä 63/2001. [*The Use of Mobile Services in 2001*, in Finnish]

Fortunati, Leopoldina. 2002. "Italy: Stereotypes, True and False." In Katz, James E., and Mark Aakhus, eds. *Perpetual Contact. Mobile Communication, Private Talk, Public Performance*. Cambridge: Cambridge University Press.

———, and Anna Maria Manganelli. 2002. "Young People and the Mobile Telephone." *Revista de estudios de juventud* 57: 59–78.

———, James E. Katz, and Raimonda Riccini, eds. 2003. *Mediating the Human Body. Technology, Communication, and Fashion*. Mahwah, NJ: Lawrence Erlbaum.

Francis, David, and Christopher Hart. 1997. "Narrative Intelligibility and Membership Categorization in a Television Commercial." In Hester, Stephen, and Peter Eglin, eds. *Culture in Action. Studies in Membership Categorization Analysis*. Washington, D.C.: International Institute for Ethnomethodology and Conversation Analysis and University Press of America.

Frohlich, David. 2004. 2004. *Audiophotography. Bringing Photos to Life with Sounds.* London: Kluwer.

———, and Ella Tallyn. 1999. "Audiophotograpy: Practice and Prospects. *Proceedings of Computer-Human Interaction CHI'99,* May 15–20. New York: ACM Library.

———, Allan Kuchinsky, Celine Pering, Abbe Don, and Steven Ariss. 2002. "Requirements for Photoware." *Proceedings of Computer-Supported Collaborative Work CSCW'02,* New Orleans, Louisiana, November 16–20.

Gardner, Sandra. 1991. "Exploring the Family Album: Social Class Differences in Images of Family Life." *Sociological Inquiry* 61: 242–251.

Garfinkel, Harold. 1957. "Conditions of Status Degradation Ceremonies." *American Journal of Sociology* 61: 420–424.

———. 1967. *Studies in Ethnomethodology.* Englewood Cliffs, NJ: Prentice-Hall.

———. 1975. "The Origins of the Term 'Ethnomethodology.'" In Turner, Roy, ed. *Ethnomethodology.* Harmondsworth: Penguin.

———, ed. 1986. *Ethnomethodological Studies of Work.* London: Routledge and Kegan Paul.

———. 1996. "Ethnomethodology's Program." *Social Psychology Quarterly* 59: 5–21.

———. 2002. *Ethnomethodogy's Program. Working Out Durkheim's Aphorism.* Lanham, MD: Rowman and Littlefield.

Geertz, Clifford. 1973. "Thick Description. Towards an Interpretive Theory of Culture." In Geertz, Clifford. *The Interpretation of Cultures.* New York: Basic Books.

Gergen, Kenneth. 2002. "The Challenge of Absent Presence." In Katz, James E., and Mark Aakhus, eds. *Perpetual Contact. Mobile Communication, Private Talk, Public Performance.* Cambridge: Cambridge University Press.

———. 2007. "Mobile Communication and the Transformation of Democratic Process." In Katz, James, ed. *Mainstreaming Mobiles: Mobile Communication and Social Change.* Cambridge. MA: The MIT Press (forthcoming)

Gibson, James. 1979. *The Ecological Approach to Visual Perception.* Boston: Houghton Mifflin.

Goffman, Erving. 1967. *Interaction Ritual. Essays on Face-to-Face Behavior.* New York: Pantheon.

———. 1981. *Forms of Talk.* Philadelphia: University of Pennsylvania Press.

Goodwin, Charles. 1981. *Conversational Organization. Interaction between Speakers and Hearers.* New York: Academic Press.

———. 1994. "Professional Vision." *American Anthropologist* 96: 606–633.

———. 1995. "Seeing in Depth." *Social Studies of Science* 25: 237–274.

———, and Marjorie Harness Goodwin. 1987. "Concurrent Operations on Talk: Notes on the Interactive Organization of Assessments." *IPRA Papers in Pragmatics* 1: 1–54.

———, and Marjorie Harness Goodwin. 1996. "Seeing as Situated Activity: Formulating Planes." In Engeström, Yrjö, and David Middleton, eds. *Cognition and Communication at Work.* Cambridge: Cambridge University Press.

Goodwin, Marjorie Harness. 1990. *He-Said-She-Said.* Bloomington: Indiana University Press.

Grinter, Rebecca E., and Margery Eldridge. 2001. "'Y do tngrs luv 2 txt msg?'" In Prinz, W., M. Jarke, Y. Rogers, K. Schmidt, and V. Wulf, eds. *Proceedings of the Seventh European Conference on Computer-Supported Cooperative Work EC-SCW'01,* 219–238. Bonn, Germany. Dordrecht, Netherlands: Kluwer.

———. 2003. "Wan2tlk?: Everyday Text Messaging." *Proceedings of Computer-Human Interaction CHI'03,* Ft. Lauderdale, Florida, April 5–10.

Gross, Edward S., and Gregory P. Stone. 1964. "Embarrassment and the Analysis of Role Requirements." *American Journal of Sociology* 70: 1–15.

Gurwitsch, Aron. 1964. *The Field of Consciousness*. Pittsburgh, PA: Duquesne University Press.

Habuchi, Ichiyo. 2005. "Accelerating Reflexivity." In Ito, Mizuko, Daisuke Okabe, and Misa Matsuda, eds. *Personal, Portable, Pedestrian. Mobile Phones in Japanese Life*. Cambridge, MA: The MIT Press.

Halle, David. 1993. *Inside Culture. Art and Class in the American Home*. Chicago: University of Chicago Press.

Hannerz, Ulf. 1967. "Gossip, Networks and Culture in a Black American Ghetto." *Ethnos* 32: 35–60.

Harper, Richard. 2003. "Are Mobiles Good of Bad for Society?" In Nyíri, Kristóf, ed. *Mobile Democracy. Essays on Society, Self and Politics*. Vienna: Passagen Verlag.

———, Leysia Palen, and Alex Taylor, eds. 2005. *The Inside Text. Social, Cultural and Design Perspectives on SMS*. Dordrecht: Springer.

Heath, Christian, and Paul Luff. 2000. *Technology in Action*. Cambridge University Press, Cambridge.

———, Paul Luff, Dirk vom Lehn, Jon Hindmarsh, and Jason Cleverly. 2002a. "Crafting Participation. Designing Ecologies, Configuring Experience." *Visual Communication* 1: 9–34.

Heath, Christian, Paul Luff, and Marcus Sanchez-Svensson. 2002b. "Overseeing Organizations. Configuring Action and Its Environment." *British Journal of Sociology* 53: 181–201.

Hester, Stephen, and Peter Eglin. 1997. "Membership Categorization Analysis: An Introduction." In Hester, Stephen, and Peter Eglin, eds. *Culture in Action. Studies in Membership Categorization Analysis*. Washington, D.C.: International Institute for Ethnomethodology and Conversation Analysis and University Press of America.

Heritage, John. 1989. *Garfinkel and Ethnomethodology*. London: Polity.

Hewitt, John P., and Randall Stokes. 1975. "Disclaimers" *American Sociological Review* 40: 1–11.

Höflich, Joachim, and Patrick Rössler. 2002. "More than JUST a Telephone: The Mobile Phone and Use of the Short Message Service (SMS) by German Adolescents: Results of a Pilot Study." *Revista de estudios de juventud* 57: 79–100.

Holly, Werner, Ulrich Püschel, Jörg Bergmann, eds. 2001. *Der sprechende Zuschauer. Wie wir uns Fernsehen kommunikativ aneignen*. Wiesbaden: Westdeutscher Verlag.

Hosokawa, Shuhei. 1984. "The Walkman Effect." *Popular Music* 4: 165–180.

Hughes, Thomas P. 1983. *Networks of Power. Electrification in Western Society 1880–1930*. Baltimore, MD: Johns Hopkins University Press.

Hung, Shin-Yuan, Cheng-Yan Ku, and Chia-Ming Chang. 2003. "Critical Factors of WAP Services Adoption: An Empirical Study." *Electronic Commerce Research and Applications* 2: 42–60.

Hymes, Dell. 1964. "Introduction: Towards Ethnographies of Communication." In Gumpertz, John, and Dell Hymes, eds. The Ethnography of Communication. *American Anthropologist* 66: 1–34.

Ihde, Don. 1976. *Listening and Voice. A Phenomenology of Sound*. Athens: Ohio University Press.

Ishii, Kenichi. 2004. "Internet Use via Mobile Phone in Japan." *Telecommunications Policy* 28: 43–58.

Ito, Mizuko. 2004. "A New Set of Social Rules for a Newly Wireless Society." *Japan Media Review*. Annenberg School for Communication, USC. Retrieved April 15, 2004, from http://ojr.org/japan/wireless/1062208524.php.

———. 2005. Intimate Visual Co-Presence. Presented at the Workshop Pervasive Image Capture and Sharing: New Social Practices and Implications for Technology at

Ubicomp'05, Tokyo, September 11-14. Retrieved September 20, 2005, from http://ubicomp.org/ubicomp2005.

Jacucci, Giulio, Antti Oulasvirta, and Antti Salovaara. 2006. "Active Construction of Experience through Mobile Media. A Field Study with Implications for Recording and Sharing." *Personal and Ubiquitous Computing* (forthcoming).

Jayysi, Lena. 1984. *Categorization and the Moral Order*. Boston: Routledge & Kegan Paul.

Jefferson, Gail. 1984. "Transcript Notation." In Atkinson, J. Maxwell, and John Heritage, eds. *Structures of Social Action. Studies in Conversation Analysis*. Cambridge: Cambridge University Press.

———. 1988. "On the Sequential Organization of Troubles-Talk in Ordinary Conversation." *Social Problems* 35: 418–441.

Johnsen, Truls E. 2000. *Ring meg! En studie av ungdom og mobiltelefoni*. Department of Ethnology, University of Oslo, Oslo. [*Call Me! A Study of Youth and Mobile Telephony*, in Norwegian]

———. 2003. "The Social Context of the Mobile Phone Use of Norwegian Teens." In Fortunati, Leopondina, James E. Katz, and Raimonda Riccini, eds. *Mediating the Human Body: Technology, Communication and Fashion*. 161–170. London: Lawrence Earlbaum.

Kaplan, Abraham. 1964. *The Conduct of Inquiry*. San Francisco: Chandler.

Kasesniemi, Eija-Liisa. 2003. *Mobile Messages. Young People and New Communication Culture*. Vammala: University of Tampere Press.

———, Ari Ahonen, Tiina Kymäläinen, and Tytti Virtanen. 2003. *Elävän mobiilikuvan ensi tallenteet. Käyttäjien kokemuksia videoviestinnästä*. Espoo: VTT Tiedotteita 2204.

Katz, James E. 2005. "Mobile Phones in Educational Settings." In Nyíri, Kristóf, ed. *A Sense of Place*. Vienna: Passagen-Verlag.

———, and Mark Aakhus. 2002. "Introduction." In Katz, James E, and Mark Aakhus, eds. *Perpetual Contact. Mobile Communication, Private Talk, Public Performance*. Cambridge: Cambridge University Press.

Kendon, Adam. 2004. *Gesture. Visible Action as Utterance*. Cambridge: Cambridge University Press.

Kindberg, Tim, Mirjana Spasojevic, Rowenta Fleck, and Abigail Sellen 2004. *How and Why People Use Camera Phones*. Consumer Applications and Systems Laboratory. H&P Laboratories Bristol, HPL-2004-216, November 26. H&P Web site: http://hp.com.

Kopomaa, Timo. 2000. *The City in Your Pocket. Birth of the Mobile Information Society*. Helsinki: Gaudeamus.

Koskinen, Ilpo. 2003. "User-Generated Content in Mobile Multimedia: Empirical Evidence from User Studies." *Proceedings of International Conference of Multimedia and Expo ICME'03*, IEEE Publication, Baltimore, Maryland.

———. 2005a. "Seeing with Mobile Images." In Nyíri, Kristof, ed. *A Sense of Place*. Vienna: Passagen-Verlag.

———. 2007a. "Managing Banality in Mobile Multimedia." In Pertierra, Raul, ed. *The Social Construction and Usage of Communication Technologies. Asian and European Perspectives. Manila: The University of the Philippines Press.*

———. 2005b. "How People Use Sound in Mobile Multimedia." *Proceedings of DPPI 2005: Designing Pleasurable Products and Interfaces*, TU/Eindhoven, October 24–28, Eindhoven, the Netherlands.

———. 2006. "Mobile Multimedia: Uses and Social Consequences." In Katz, James, ed. *A Handbook of Mobile Communication and Social Change*. Cambridge. MA: The MIT Press (forthcoming).

————, Esko Kurvinen, and Turo-Kimmo Lehtonen. 2002. *Mobile Image*. Helsinki: IT Press.

————, and Esko Kurvinen. 2002. "Messages visuels mobiles. Nouvelle technologie et interaction." *Réseaux: communication, technologie, société* n° 112–113: 107–138.

————, and Esko Kurvinen. 2005. "Mobile Multimedia and Users: The Domestication of Mobile Multimedia." *Telektronikk* 101 (3–4): 60–68.

————, Pertti Alasuutari, and Tuomo Peltonen. 2005a. *Laadulliset menetelmät kauppatieteissä*. Tampere: Vastapaino [*Qualitative Methods in Business Studies*, in Finnish].

————, Seppo Väkevä, and Esko Kurvinen. 2005b. "How to Study Mobile Multimedia on the Air. The Internet as an Observational Instrument." Presented in Workshop "Fieldwork Untethered," November 2005, Keio University, Tokyo.

Kurvinen, Esko. 2002. "Emotions in Action: A Case in Mobile Visual Communication." *Proceedings of the 3rd International Design and Emotion Conference* D+E'02.

————. 2003. "Only When Miss Universe Snatches Me. Teasing in MMS Messaging." *Proceeding of Designing Pleasurable Products and Interfaces DPPI'03*, June 23–26, 2003, Pittsburgh, Pennsylvania.

————. 2007. *Prototyping Social*. Helsinki: University of Art and Design (forthcoming).

————, Katja Battarbee, and Ilpo Koskinen. 2006. "Prototyping Social Interaction." *Design Issues* (forthcoming).

Kusahara, Machiko. 2004. Mobile Culture in Japan. Lecture at the University of Art and Design, Helsinki, Finland, September 9.

Latour, Bruno. 1987. *Science in Action. How to Follow Scientists and Engineers Through Society*. Milton Keynes: Open University Press.

Laursen, Ditte. 2005. "Please Reply! The Replying Norm in Adolescent SMS Communication." In Harper, Richard, Leysia Palen, and Alex Taylor, eds. *The Inside Text. Social, Cultural and Design Perspectives on SMS*. Dordrecht: Springer.

————. 2006. *Det mobile samtalerum*. Ph.D. diss. Sønderborg: Institut for sprog og kommunikation, Syddansk universitet [*Mobile conversation*, in Danish].

Lehtonen, Turo-Kimmo, Ilpo Koskinen, and Esko Kurvinen. 2003. Mobile Digital Pictures—the Future of the Postcard? Findings from an Experimental Field Study. Presented at The 9th Interdisciplinary Conference on Research in Consumption. Department of Design History/Material Culture, University of Applied Arts, Vienna, Austria, June 27–29.

Licoppe, Christian, and Jean-Philippe Heurtin. 2001. "Managing One's Availability to Telephone Communication through Mobile Phones. A French Case Study of the Development Dynamics of Mobile Phone Use." *Personal and Ubiquitous Computing* 5: 99–108.

————. 2004. "Connected Presence. The Emergence of a New Repertoire for Managing Social Relationships in a Changing Communication Technoscape." *Environment and Planning D: Society and Space* 22: 135–156.

Ling, Rich. 2003. "Fashion and Vulgarity in the Adoption of the Mobile Telephone among Teens in Norway." In Fortunati, Leopoldina, James E. Katz, and Raimonda Riccini, eds. *Mediating the Human Body. Technology, Communication, and Fashion*. Mahwah, NJ: Lawrence Erlbaum.

————. 2004. *The Mobile Connection*. San Francisco: Morgan Kaufmann.

————. 2006. "Mediated Ritual Interaction and the Mobile Telephone." In Katz, James, ed. *Mainstreaming Mobiles: Mobile Communication and Social Change*. Cambridge. MA: The MIT Press (forthcoming).

————, and Tom Julsrud. 2005. "The Development of Grounded Genres in Multimedia Messaging Systems (MMS) among Mobile Professionals." To appear in Nyíri, Kristof, ed. *A Sense of Place*. Vienna: Passagen-Verlag.

Lobet-Maris, Claire. 2003. "Mobile Phone Tribes. Youth and Social Identity." In Fortunati, Leopoldina, James E. Katz, and Raimonda Riccini, eds. *Mediating the Human Body. Technology, Communication, and Fashion.* Mahwah, NJ: Lawrence Erlbaum.
―――, and Jaurent Henin. 2002. "Talking Without Communicating or Communicating Without Talking: From the GSM to the SMS." *Revista de estudios de juventud* 57: 101–114.
Lorente, Santiago. 2002. Special Number on "Youth and Mobile Telephones." *Revista de estudios de juventud* 57 (juny).
Mäkelä, Anu, Verena Giller, Manfred Tscheligi, and Reinhard Sefelin. 2000. "Joking, Storytelling, Artsharing, Expressing Affection: A Field Trial of How Children and Their Social Network Communicate with Digital Images in Leisure Time." *Proceedings of Computer-Human Interaction CHI'00: Human Factors in Computing Systems.* New York: ACM Press, April.
Mante-Meijer, Enid A., and Dóris Pires. 2002. "SMS Use by Young People in the Netherlands." *Revista de estudios de juventud* 57: 47–58.
Margolis, J. 2005. *Mob-log. Scenes from My Mobile.* London: Artnik books.
Matsunaga, Mari. 2000. *i-mode. The Birth of i-mode.* Singapore: Chuang Yi Publishers.
Maynard, Douglas W. 1984. *Inside Plea Bargaining: The Language of Negotiation.* New York: Plenum.
Merleau-Ponty, Maurice. 1986. *Phenomenology of Perception.* London: Routledge and Kegan Paul.
Merton, Robert. 1968. "Manifest and Latent Functions." In Merton, Robert K. *Social Theory and Social Structure.* New York: The Free Press.
Metso, Antero, Minna Isomursu, Pekka Isomursu, and Lassi Tasajärvi. 2004. "Classification of Mobile Micromovies." Proceedings of the 2004 IEEE International Conference on Multimedia and Expo, ICME 2004, Taipei, Taiwan, June 27-30.
Miller, Daniel, and Don Slater. 2000. *The Internet. An Ethnographic Approach.* Oxford: Berg.
Murray, Janet H. 1999. *Hamlet on the Holodeck. The Future of Narrative in Cyberspace.* Cambridge, MA: The MIT Press.
Natsuno, Takeshi. 2003. *i-mode Strategy.* Chichester: John Wiley & Sons.
Negroponte, Nicholas. 1999. *Being Digital.* New York: Vintage.
Nielsen, Jacob. 1993. *Usability Engineering.* San Francisco: Morgan Kaufmann.
Noguchi, Yuki. 2005. "Camera Phones Lend Immediacy to Images of Disaster." *Washington Post*, July 8, p. A16. Retrieved September 30, 2005, from http://washingtonpost.com.
Nurmela, Juha, Risto Heinonen, Pauli Ollila, and Vesa Virtanen. 2000. *Mobile Phones and Computers as Parts of Everyday Life in Finland.* Helsinki: Statistics Finland, Reviews 2000/5.
―――, Lea Parjo, and Marko Ylitalo. 2003. *A Great Migration to the Information Society. Patterns of ICE Diffusion in Finland in 1996-2002.* Helsinki: Statistics Finland, Reviews 2003/1.
Nyíri, Kristóf. 2003. "Pictorial Meaning and Mobile Communication." In Nyíri, Kristóf, ed. *Mobile Communication. Essays on Cognition and Community.* Vienna: Passagen Verlag.
Ochs, Elinor, Sally Jacoby, and Patrick Gonzales. 1994. Interpretive Journeys. How Physicists Talk and Travel through Graphic Space." *Configurations* 1: 151–171.
O'Hara, Kenton, Alison Black, and Matthew Lipson. 2006. "Everyday Practices with Mobile Video Technology." *Proceedings of Computer-Human Interaction, CHI 2006,* Montréal, Québec, Canada, April 22-27.

Ok, HyeRyoung. 2005. "Cinema in Your Hand, Cinema on the Street: The Aesthetics of Convergence in Korean Mobile(phone) Cinema." *Proceedings of Seeing, Understanding. Learning in the Mobile Age. Communications in the 21st Century: The Mobile Information Society*, Budapest, Hungary, April 28–30.

Okabe, Daisuke. 2004. "Emergent Social Practices, Situations and Relations through Everyday Camera Phone Use." *Proceedings of Mobile Communication and Social Change, 2004 International Conference on Mobile Communication*, Seoul, Korea, October 18–19.

———, and Mizuko Ito. 2004. "Camera Phones Changing the Definition of Picture-Worthy." *Japan Media Review*. Annenberg School for Communication, USC. http://ojr.org/japan/wireless/1062208524.php. Accessed April 15, 2004.

———, and Mizuko Ito. 2006. "Everyday Contexts of Camera Phone Use: Steps Toward Technosocial Ethnographic Frameworks." In Höflich, Joachim, and Maren Hartmann, eds. *Mobile Communication in Everyday Life: An Ethnographic View*. Berlin: Frank & Timme.

Okada, Tomoyuki. 2005. "Youth Culture and the Shaping of Japanese Mobile Media: Personalization and the *Keitai* Internet as Multimedia." In Ito, Mizuko, Daisuke Okabe, and Misa Matsuda, eds. *Personal, Portable, Pedestrian*. Cambridge, MA: The MIT Press.

Orr, Julian. 1990. "Sharing Knowledge, Celebrating Identity. Community Memory in a Service Culture." In Middleton, David, and Derek Edwards, eds. *Collective Remembering*. London: Sage.

———. 1996. *Talking about Machines. An Ethnography of a Modern Job*. Ithaca, NY: Cornell University Press and ILR Press.

Parsons, Talcott. 1937. *The Structure of Social Action*. New York: McGraw Hill.

Pertierra, Raul, Eduardo F. Ugarte, Alicia Pingol, Joel Hernandez, and Nikos Lexis Dacanay. 2002. *Txt-ing Selves. Cellphones and Philippine Modernity*. Manila: De La Salle University Press.

Pomerantz, Anita. 1984. "Agreeing and Disagreeing with Assessments: Some Features of Preferred/Dispreferred Turn Shapes." In J. Maxwell Atkinson and John Heritage, eds. *Structures of Social Action. Studies in Conversation Analysis*. Cambridge: Cambridge University Press.

Popper, Karl. 1963. *Conjectures and Refutations. The Growth of Scientific Knowledge*. London: Routledge.

Ratliff, John M. 2001. "NTT DoCoMo and Its i-mode Success. Origins and Implications." *California Management Review* 44: 55–71.

Relieu, Marc. 2002. The "Glasscam" as an Observational Tool for Studying Screen-Based Mobile Phone Uses and Management of Parallel Activities. Paper presented at The International Conference on Conversation Analysis ICCA-2002. Copenhagen, Denmark, June.

Repo, Petteri, Kaarina Hyvönen, Mika Pantzar, and Päivi Timonen. 2003. *Mobile Video*. Helsinki: National Consumer Research Centre. Publications 2003: 5. Available at http://ncrc.fi.

Rheingold, Howard. 2003a. *Smart Mobs. The Next Social Revolution*. Cambridge, MA: Perseus.

———. 2003b. "Moblogs Seen as a Crystal Ball for a New Era in Online Journalism." *Online Journalism Review*. Retrieved October 1, 2005, from http://ojr.org/ojr/technology/1057780670.php.

Rice, Ronald E., and James E. Katz. 2003. "Comparing Internet and Mobile Phone Usage. Digital Divides of Usage, Adoption, and Dropouts." *Telecommunications Policy* 27: 597–623.

Rivière, Carole-Anne. 2002. "Mini-Messaging in Everyday Interactions. A Dual Strategy for Exteriorising and Hiding Privacy to Maintain Social Contacts." *Revista de estudios de juventud* 57: 125–138.

———. 2005. "Seeing and Writing on a Mobile Phone: New Forms of Sociability in Interpersonal Communications." *Proceedings of Seeing, Understanding, Learning in the Mobile Age. Communications in the 21st Century: The Mobile Information Society*, Budapest, Hungary, April 28–30.

Sacks, Harvey. 1972a. "On the Analyzability of Stories by Children." In Gumperz, John J., and Dell Hymes, eds. *Directions in Sociolinguistics: The Ethnography of Communication*. New York: Holt, Reinhart and Winston.

———. 1972b. "An Initial Investigation of the Usability of Conversational Data for Doing Sociology." In Sudnow, David N., ed. *Studies in Social Interaction*. New York: The Free Press.

———. 1984. "Notes on Methodology." In Atkinson, J. Maxwell, and John Heritage, eds. *Structures of Social Action. Studies in Conversation Analysis*. Cambridge: Cambridge University Press.

———. 1995. *Lectures on Conversations*. Two volumes. Cambridge: Blackwell.

———, Emanuel A. Schegloff, and Gail Jefferson. 1974. "A Simplest Systematics for the Organization of Turn Taking in Conversation." *Language* 50: 696–735.

———, and Emanuel A. Schegloff. 1979. "Two Preferences in the Organization of Reference to Persons in Conversation and Their Interaction." In Phatsas, George, ed. *Everyday Language. Studies in Ethnomethodology*. New York: John Wiley & Sons.

Salovaara, Antti, Giulio Jacucci, Antti Oulasvirta, Timo Saari, Pekka Kanerva, Esko Kurvinen, Sauli Tiitta. 2006. "Collective Creation and Sense-Making of Mobile Media." *Proceedings of Computer-Human Interaction, CHI 2006*, Montréal, Québec, Canada, April 22–27.

Samtani, Anil, Leow Tze Ting, Lim Hoon Moe, Goh Po Gin Jonathan. 2003. "Overcoming Barriers fop the Successful Adoption of Mobile Commerce in Singapore". *International Journal of Mobile Communication* 1: 194–231.

Schegloff, Emanuel A. 1972. "Notes on a Conversational Practice: Formulating Place." In Sudnow, David, ed. *Studies in Social Interaction*. 75–119. New York: The Free Press.

———. 1986. "The Routine as Achievement." *Human Studies* 9: 111–52.

———. 1992. "On Talk and Its Institutional Occasions." In Drew, Paul, and John Heritage, eds. *Talk at Work. Interaction in Institutional Settings*. Cambridge: Cambridge University Press.

———, and Harvey Sacks 1973. "Opening up Closings." *Semiotica* 8: 289–327.

Schnaars, Steve, and Cliff Wymbs. 2004." On the Persistence of Lackluster Demans. The History of the Video Telephone." *Technological Forecasting and Social Change* 71: 197-216.

Scifo, Barbara. 2005. "The Domestication of the Camera Phone and MMS Communications. The Experience of Young Italians." In K. Nyíri, ed. *A Sense of Place*. Vienna: Passagen-Verlag.

Scott, Marvin B., and Scott Lyman. 1968. "Accounts." *American Sociological Review* 33: 46–62.

Seale, Clive. 1999. *The Quality of Qualitative Data*. London: Sage.

Sharrock, Wes, and Graham Button. 1993. "Epistemology: Professional Skepticism." In Button, Graham, ed. *Ethnomethodology and the Human Sciences*. Cambridge: Cambridge University Press.

Smith, Dorothy E. 1984. "Textually Mediated Social Organization." *International Social Science Journal* 36: 59–75.

Smith, Sidonie, and Julia Watson, eds. 1996. *Getting a Life: Everyday Uses of Autobiography*. Minneapolis: University of Minnesota Press.

Suchman, Lucy. 1987. *Plans and Situated Actions*. Cambridge: University of Cambridge Press.

Tainio, Liisa. 1999. "Postikortti työpaikalle" [A Postcard to the Workplace]. In Laakso, Ville, and Jan-Ola Östman, eds. *Postikortti diskurssina*. [Postcard as Discourse in Finnish]. Hämeenlinna: Korttien talo.

Taylor, Alex S., and Richard Harper. 2002. "Age-Old Practices in the "New World": A Study of Gift-Giving Between Teenage Mobile Phone Users." 439–446. *Proceedings of Computer-Human Interaction CHI'02*, Minneapolis, Minnesota, April 20–25.

————. 2003. "The Gift of the Gab? A Design Oriented Sociology of Young People's Use of Mobiles." *Computer Supported Cooperative Work* 12: 267-296.

Teo, Thompson S. H., and Siau Heong Pok. 2003a. "Adoption of WAP-Enabled Mobile Phones among Internet Users." *Omega* 31: 483–498.

————. 2003b. "Adoption of the Internet and WAP-Enabled Phones in Singapore." *Behavior and Information Technology* 22: 281–289.

Terasaki, Alene K. 1976. *Pre-Announcement Sequences in Conversation*. Irvine: University of California, Irvine, School of Social Sciences. Social Science Working Paper 99.

Thibaud, Jean-Paul. 2003. "The Sonic Composition of the City." In Bull, Michael, and Les Back, eds. *The Auditory Culture Reader*. Oxford: Berg.

Ulkuniemi, Seija. 1998. "Kuvitella elämää. Perhevalokuvan lajityypin tarkastelua" [Imagining Living: Studying the Genre of Home Photography in Finnish] Licentiate's thesis. Rovaniemi: University of Lapland, The Faculty of Art and Design.

van House, Nancy, and Marc Davis. 2005. The Social Life of Cameraphone Images. Presented at the Workshop Pervasive Image Capture and Sharing: New Social Practices and Implications for Technology at *Ubicomp'05*, Shinagawa, Tokyo, September 11-14. Retrieved September 20, 2005, from http://ubicomp.org/ubicomp2005.

vom Lehn, Dirk, Christian Heath, and Jon Hindmarsh. 2001. "Exhibiting Interaction: Conduct and Collaboration in Museums and Galleries." *Symbolic Interaction* 24: 189–216.

Weilenmann, Alexandra, and Catrine Larsson. 2001. "Local Use and Sharing of Mobile Phones." In Brown, Barry, Nicola Green, and Richard Harper, eds. *Wireless World. Social and Interactional Aspects of the Mobile Age*. London: Springer.

Wilson, Tom. 1991. "Social Structure and the Sequential Organization of Interaction." In Boden, Deirdre, and Don H. Zimmerman, eds. *Talk and Social Structure. Studies in Ethnomethodology and Conversation Analysis*. Berkeley: University of California Press.

Yerkovich, Sally. 1976. "Gossiping; Or, The Creation of Fictional Lives, Being a Study of the Subject in an Urban American Setting Drawing upon Vignettes from Upper Middle Class Lives." Ph.D. diss., University of Pennsylvania, Department of Folklore and Folklife.

Zimmerman, Don H., and Melvin Pollner. 1990. "The Everyday World as a Phenomenon" In McKinney, J. C., and E. A. Tiryakin, eds. *Theoretical Sociology: Perspectives and Developments*. Reprinted in Coulter, Jeff, ed. 1990. *Ethnomethodological Sociology*. Great Yarmouth: Galliard. An Elgar Reference Collection. Original version in 1970.

Subject Index

Name Index